LANCE ARMSTRONG FOUNDATION

LIVESTRONG™

INSPIRATIONAL STORIES FROM CANCER SURVIVORS:
FROM DIAGNOSIS TO TREATMENT AND BEYOND

BANTAM
SYDNEY AUCKLAND TORONTO NEW YORK LONDON

LIVE STRONG
A BANTAM BOOK

First published in the United States by Broadway Books in 2005
First published in Australia and New Zealand by Bantam in 2005

Transworld Publishers,
a division of Random House Australia Pty Ltd
20 Alfred Street, Milsons Point, NSW 2061
http://www.randomhouse.com.au

Random House New Zealand Limited
18 Poland Road, Glenfield, Auckland

Transworld Publishers,
a division of The Random House Group Ltd.
61-63 Uxbridge Road, Ealing, London W5 5SA

Random House Inc
1745 Broadway, New York, New York 10036

National Library of Australia
Cataloguing-in-Publication Entry

Live strong.

    ISBN 1 86325 581 8.

    1. Cancer – Patients – Biography. I. Armstrong, Lance.
    II. Lance Armstrong Foundation.

    362.19699400922

Cover photograph by Michael N. Heiko
Cover design by Rex Bonomelli
Printed and bound by Griffin Press, Netley, South Australia

10 9 8 7 6 5 4 3 2 1

Contents

Introduction

LANCE**ARMSTRONG**

Like winning the Tour de France, my recovery from cancer was not something I accomplished on my own. My progress was helped along by my doctors and nurses, my family—especially my mother—my friends, teammates, fans, and fellow survivors. But what I found was that, even with their support, I wanted tools to help me be in control of the experience. I wanted numbers, statistics, data: things that could be measured. I wanted to be as educated as possible because the statistics show that the more knowledge cancer patients have, the better their chances of survival. But it was hard to find the information I was looking for. I spent hours upon hours of searching the Internet, reading books, and bothering my doctors.

After I was in remission, I had the feeling that my cancer was "over." I felt like I was supposed to get on with my life, pick up where I had left off before the diagnosis. But I found that I was still thinking about my cancer a lot. I had thoughts of recurrence, thoughts of dying, thoughts that my mother and my friends who hadn't had cancer themselves couldn't truly understand or help me through. I was always worrying about my health. Things that other people might not think twice about, like a bump or an ache, made me think that my cancer was back. The slightest physical change was cause for in-depth analysis, deep pondering, phone calls to doctors, and distress.

The medical professionals could only offer me scientific evidence. They ran tests and assured me time and time again that I was fine, but I still worried. While I was fortunate to have wonderful access to many experts and resources that helped me make informed decisions about my life after diagnosis, I needed to know that answers were still being sought and new research developed. I wanted to turn my individual energy into a larger advocacy machine that could demand results, accountability, and continued commitment from the medical community as well as our government. This need inspired the creation of the Lance Armstrong Foundation. The LAF believes that in your battle with cancer, unity is strength, knowledge is power, and attitude is everything. From the moment of diagnosis, we provide the practical information and tools people with cancer need to live strong.

I also felt there might be a small chance that other people would listen to my story or maybe even benefit from hearing my story—the symptoms, the side effects of the treatment, and post-treatment life. Sharing my story was therapeutic, but I also had hopes that my experiences could help somebody else. My work with the LAF shows me daily that sharing our stories and learning from one another's experiences helps us cancer survivors continue to survive. Some people think the cancer experience is only about the diagnosis and treatment of cancer, as if after the disease goes into remission, it no longer exists. But survivorship goes beyond remission. Survivorship is an evolution. It begins on the day of diagnosis and never ends. Survivors are people with cancer. They are people whose mothers, fathers, brothers, sisters, wives, husbands, partners, friends, and co-workers are surviving cancer. Reading and listening to their stories on the LIVE**STRONG** Website, and now seeing some of them collected between the covers of this book, I am convinced once again that the LAF is meeting the needs of millions of cancer survivors. The narratives here are a sampling from those millions of other survivors throughout the world. While all of us are not fortunate (or unfortunate) enough to have our stories told around the world, I think it is important to let people everywhere know that we are an army. This is a big disease, a big problem—it affects millions of people, and we are not silent. The more people who stand up and say, "I am a cancer survivor," and the more people who tell their story, the more power we have to demand change. Each individual has a unique experience and perspective to share, and seeing these stories reminds me that there is always a larger community that I belong to. Sometimes hearing the experiences of cancer survivors or their families is a double-edged sword. You don't want to hear that someone has been diagnosed; you don't want to hear that maybe someone has died. But to hear that story can be incredibly inspiring if the person lived and went on to live a healthy and fruitful life. That inspires me, and it inspires everyone around them. On the other hand, sometimes people don't make it, and those are the stories you hate to hear. But then again, sometimes it has such an effect on a family or community or school or workplace that it still makes a big difference. Although that person is no longer there, his or her influence goes on for years and years and years. It is my hope that these stories, along with those from survivors all over the world, are shared as my story has been. My own efforts, as well as those of the others who work for the LAF, are focused on making sure that the LAF is a voice for cancer survivors. We want cancer survivors and their families to reach out and let their voices be heard and to find information of the most personal and practical kind: from advice on how to tell your kids about cancer to the tools necessary to be an effective advocate for survivorship programs. This book is just one chance to learn and listen, to hear and be heard. This book is the voice of cancer survivors, living strong.

LANCE ARMSTRONG FOUNDATION

LIVESTRONG™

"I am somebody with cancer and I am somebody without cancer."

SAMANTHA**EISENSTEIN**

I became a survivor when I was diagnosed with Ewing's sarcoma in December of 1999.

I went down to New York for treatment and started in January of 2000. Treatment went through September of 2000 with seven rounds of high-dose chemo and surgery. The tumor was in my leg, in the tibia. I spent about four months at home afterward, September through December, recovering with physical therapy. I was a senior in college when I was diagnosed and only had one semester left. I went back to school in January of 2001 and was always tired, always bruising, and always catching everything that was going around. Because of the high-dose chemo that I got, I kept going in for tests, but the doctors just kept saying, "Your bone marrow is tired. It'll start working. It's just working slowly." Finally, I went in for a bone-marrow biopsy in April of 2001 and they found the secondary myelodysplastic syndrome, which is one of the precursors to leukemia. I said to them, "If there is anything I can be doing from now until May when I graduate, I'll do it, but otherwise, leave me alone. I want to go back to school." I knew that the search for a bone-marrow donor could be long and drawn out. They said that was fine. So I went back and graduated from college in May of 2001. I started chemo again in June or July to get the disease back into remission, because it had started to progress. I was home for a couple of weeks and they found a perfect donor match for me. All they told me was that he was young and male. I found out later he's from St. Louis, but I haven't met him yet. I underwent the bone-marrow transplant in August of 2001, was in the hospital for three months, spent the nine months afterward going in for tests and medications and anti-rejection and anti-everything drugs, and finally in June of 2002, they said, "Okay. You're set. Go do your thing." So I went up to graduate school at Middlebury College for the summer and moved to Boston in September of 2002. I started working for a public-health-education nonprofit where we do mostly HIV-prevention research, and interventions and violence prevention.

Then last year I went to the I'm Too Young for This symposium that was held at MIT. It was the first time I even found out that there were other young-adult survivors, because in a hospital like the one I was treated in, sadly, nobody ever really left. All of my friends had passed away. I didn't have any people that I went through treatment with who made it long enough to go through the survivorship journey with me. Since I finished, I had been struggling with my appearance and scars, all the issues that are not the day-to-day chemo stuff and therefore didn't feel legitimate. But I went to that conference and saw that there was a whole community of people like me out there. The keynote speaker talked about how he gets approached by so many survivors who say, "I need to quit my job. I don't know what I want to do, but this is where I want to be." And I realized that's exactly how I felt. So my friend Bridget and I started talking about organizing a benefit concert for young-adult survivors to help them transition out of treatment and into the "real world." We started doing research and found that there aren't any organizations designed to provide educational scholarships, professional training, and advice on rent, loans, car payments, grocery and residual medical bills for young-adult survivors. But instead of being discouraged and giving up completely, we gave up the idea of the benefit concert and just decided to go full steam ahead and create our own organization. It's called Surviving and Moving Forward. It's called the SAM Fund for young adult survivors of cancer. I feel uncomfortable saying, "I'm Sam, and this is the SAM Fund," because though it did start obviously from my own story and experiences, the acronym comes from Surviving and Moving Forward. We want to help people who are no longer receiving treatment and feel abandoned. When I was going through treatment, all the doctors and nurses were focused on getting me to the day when they would tell me that I didn't have to come back anymore. Obviously, that's a huge and important day, but then I felt that people sort of forgot about me. Being a young adult who had to go out and fend for myself, and decide either to go back to school or not, or to get a job and start paying rent, was incredibly overwhelming. It's just hard. It's hard for anybody right out of college. But then you add $20,000 in medical bills to it and it makes it even harder. And so what we decided to do was create an organization just to provide financial assistance in that transitional time.

So that's what I've been doing for the last nine months. It's been the best thing in my own cancer journey because it's given me a way to reclaim control over the whole thing, to have cancer in my life because I chose to put it there, not the other way around. It's been really empowering and really exciting. I've met some amazing people. We've already started partnering with other organizations. We've done some fund-raising. We're working on a whole bunch of stuff. I'm actually about to go part-time at my day job, so that I can run the fund two days a week. I hope to make it full-time eventually. It's been interesting to see how all of the pieces are now coming into place. I have this incredible energy and excitement to get this fund off the ground and hand out the first check to a survivor who needs it. For that, I am very grateful. I just decided I'm going to start an MBA program for people involved with organizations or who want to be involved with organizations with a good social mission. Cancer isn't who I am, but it is where I've

been. It's a part of who I am. And to now be able to incorporate that into a career and into a positive presence in my life
makes me feel grateful.

I'm monitored long-term by an endocrinologist. When I saw
him for the first time, his nurses sat with me, listed all of the
drugs I had been on—many I had forgotten about—and said,
"Here's the risk of this disease. Here's the risk of this recurrence. You're at elevated risk for this. There's a good chance
you're going to get this." I could have heart problems, kidney
problems, liver problems, thyroid problems. Basically anything
in my body can be affected long-term by the chemo, especially
because I had five drugs in very high doses the first time
around. On top of that, I had three or four drugs in very high
doses the second time, plus all the radiation from the X-rays. I
never had standard radiation, but all the X-rays and the CAT
scans add risks to everything. I told them that I just wanted to
know what I should look for, what I can do to prevent it, what
to do if I notice any of the warning signs. Other than that, I
wanted to be left alone. I don't want to hear it every year. I
don't want to hear what my risks are, because if there's nothing
I can do about them anyway, then I don't want to live in fear
of them.

I have a multitude of scars from all the biopsies and the
catheter in my chest. The biggest scar runs from just above my
knee to my ankle. That's the worst part for me physically. I'm
lucky in that I can pretty much still do what I want, though I
can't do anything high-impact. I can't run. I can't do anything
that's going to stress that bone. The scar is not a typical scar because they had to do a skin graft. I'm very aware of it, and how
different my skin looks there. To me it's a reminder. On some
days, it's a positive reminder of where I've been and where I
am, how hard I've worked to just be able to walk. But on other
days, it's a reminder of the fact that I had cancer, which is still a
really hard thing to process sometimes. It's a reminder that I
have limitations that I didn't have before. And that's been really

hard. But other than that, I've gotten used to telling the difference between what the doctors say I can't do and what they say I shouldn't do. There are some things that they say I probably wouldn't ever be able to do again and it's just my nature to go and prove them wrong.

I hope my orthopedic surgeon doesn't see this because he'd kill me if he knew I was saying this. But anyway, when I was coming out of surgery, he sat me down and went through this big long list of things that I might not be able to do again. Among those things he told me that I couldn't do were running and playing tennis. At first I got really upset about it and then I remembered that I hate to run, so it was really no great loss. But when he said that I couldn't play tennis, I got so upset. It's the one sport that I love and have always played. And when the doctor left, this fellow in the room, who was just wonderful, said, "You can't play competitively but you can still play. Just let it bounce twice before your return. It'll be fine." I know I can't run, because it'll break the bone. But I played tennis last summer with my mom, and I let the ball bounce twice. I didn't run after anything, but, you know, even though I wouldn't be able to play competitively again, it was fine just to play that little bit. Just being on the court and having a tennis racket in my hand after hearing his voice say, "You'll never be able to do it again," felt awesome.

One of the hardest things about moving back to Boston and starting work was that people didn't know me. They asked me all the standard questions: Where was I from? What did I do before I moved here? And I didn't want to just announce that I had come from a bone-marrow transplant and that I hadn't done anything before this job because I wasn't able to work. I didn't want cancer to be the first thing that people knew about me. So I made stuff up. I was very self-conscious about it, because I had gone through a lot of physical therapy and still walked with a little bit of a limp. My hair was still very, very short. I felt like the cancer identified me before I was able to identify myself, and that when people saw me they thought, "Oh, she had cancer." So for a while I just avoided meeting new people. I avoided going out. I stayed within my comfort zone of friends and family. I think the turning point was when I founded the SAM Fund. I'm so aware of what it's brought to my life in terms of my own recovery process, and I'm excited to tell people about that. My cancer experience sort of becomes the background of the story, where the Fund is now the focus. It's been really gratifying to turn it around that way, because instead of meeting someone new and saying, "Yeah, I had cancer. Let's talk about how much that sucked," it can be, "I had cancer and here's what I'm doing about it. Here's what I'm doing with it." It's a much different experience now than it was a year ago in terms of telling people, which is also why it was such a big deal when I went to that conference and realized that there was a whole community of people out there that I didn't have to worry about those things with. I went out to Montana last year for a Young Adult Survivors conference at Camp Māk-A-Dream, and it was the same thing. Cancer is a given, so you can go from there. It was actually very interesting for me to try and figure out who I was without the cancer as a defining characteristic, because the cancer had been the biggest part of my life for the last three years. Once I didn't have to tell people I had cancer, for a little while I didn't know what to tell people at all. I didn't want people to think of me as the girl who had cancer, but that's how I'd started to think about myself when I didn't have anything else going on in my life besides doctor's appointments, physical therapy, and that kind of stuff. So it was really interesting for me to figure out who I was without all of that. That's why Boston's such a great place to be. There are so many young people just out of college who are still figuring themselves out. I feel like even though I'm twenty-six years old, I'm very much like those kids just out of college. I'm in that transitional period, where, you know, I get to call the shots and I get to decide what makes me happy and where I want to be. It's been strange being a few years behind all of my friends who have already gone through making some of those decisions. But I think it took coming into contact with so many young-adult survivors for me to realize that I am somebody with cancer and I am somebody without cancer. I just had to figure out who that person was.

I've been pretty lucky with financial matters and employment and benefits. But it is one of the biggest issues that we deal with at the Fund. We're working on providing for residual medical bills and all that kind of stuff that some people deal with, but I never had to. My insurance covered 100 percent of my treatment, and what they didn't cover as far as out-of-pocket expenses, my family covered. When I got my job, I interviewed over the phone, so I never had to meet anyone face-to-face and explain why I walked with a limp. They didn't see me until my first day of work.

I work for a nonprofit organization that has excellent benefits. And I've never been questioned about it. I got health insurance. I had my choice of plans. My co-pay is the same as anybody else's. I have a primary-care physician who is amazing and will write me a referral for any doctor I want to see. Everything so far has just fallen into place. I've been really lucky with that. My future goal of working for the Fund full-time raises the issue of health insurance. One of our trustees, who owns his own insurance company, said that he would set it up. Even if it's a little bit more expensive than getting a group plan through a different company, I don't have to worry that I'll ever be without insurance. I'm totally aware of what a huge luxury that is. I never take it for granted. I think it will probably always be my first consideration when looking for a new job or deciding whether to go back to school. Where some people have complete freedom to take a chance and do whatever they want to do, regardless of what the health-insurance situation might be, that'll never be an option for me. But I suppose it's just one of the things you learn to work around.

I definitely get pissed off about the cancer. What happened to me, and what I've seen happen with other people, is that you go through the treatment and you don't think about it because you can't. I couldn't think about what it meant to have a life-threatening illness. I couldn't think about what would happen if a certain test came back with a different result. I just did what I had to do. And that included not only the months of treatment, but the year afterward when I was still going in for follow-up visits and tests. But then it was over and it all started to sink in. Once they said, "Okay. Go live your life. Go back to Boston and get a job," I felt this whole psychological back-lash where all of a sudden I started to realize, "I had cancer, holy shit! I had a life-threatening illness and I could have died!" It's something I still deal with.

When I was diagnosed, I never went through the "why me?" or "it's not fair" phases or anything like that. But I find myself going there now. I think about it a lot. What makes me the an-griest is that being sick totally disrupted my life at a point where it shouldn't have been disrupted. Not that there's ever a time in life when it should be, and not that anyone who goes through it deserves it or anything, but I think that there are some stages in life when it's easier to deal with. It seems like it's easier for little kids. They may have to miss some school or may be apart from their friends, but they still have a place to return to when they're done and can go back to school. And older people have a job and family to go back to. But I was in the middle of my senior year in college. I didn't even have a school to go back to. I didn't have a job to go back to. I was in this totally up-in-the-air tran-sitional time when I spent so long focusing on getting better that I didn't think about what came next. I was lucky that things fell into place, but I wonder what would have happened if I had been sick at a different time in my life. How many more choices would I have had to make? Or what other factors might have come into play in getting my first job? I'm lucky that I love my job and that I get paid well, that I'm happy where I'm living and I can pay my own bills, but that's just luck.

The other thing that makes me angry is the number of people I've lost to cancer. I've been really lucky in that my friends and my family haven't budged. They've been with me the whole time and it's been very much a team effort from the beginning. But, with the exception of three of them, all of the cancer patients who I met in my three years of treatment have passed away. That's the thing that sets me apart from everybody else I know. I was twenty-one years old when I was diagnosed the first time and I was treated in pediatrics. Everybody waits in the waiting room together. You go through treatment at the same time. You're in the hospital at the same time. And I made very, very solid friendships and bonds that I don't have with anybody else. And I think to be twenty-six years old and to have lost thirteen or fourteen people that I would honestly call friends (and that's not even counting the number of people who I just know, who are acquaintances or who I had passed by in the hospital), is a little young to know that kind of loss. And that makes me really angry. It makes me really angry that we couldn't all get through this together. That adds to the survivor's guilt that I deal with every day, which is a huge side effect that they don't tell you about. It's been really hard not to compare myself to the people who have passed away in that, you know, I feel so guilty that I'm here and they're not. What people keep telling me is that I can't see it as an either/or thing; either I'm here or they're here. But I still wonder if maybe they're not here because I am. Mostly, I'm just sad. I'm just sad that my friends aren't here; that they're not able to live their lives and that they're not able to go through this stage, too, you know, to live out their futures and their dreams. It brings me back to the Fund again. On a very personal level, the Fund allows me to keep my friends with me. Their memories are right here in the front of my brain all the time, and they're with me through every step of this.

And I guess I'm angry that there are things that I have to think about that nobody else my age does. I have to be careful of how many pounds I lift, because it might stress my heart. I have to be careful of walking too fast, because I may get a shin splint or I may hurt my leg in some way. I'm twenty-six. People my age think they're invincible, and I don't have the luxury of believing in that illusion.

Therapy is the best thing in the world. Therapy gives me a sounding board. It gives me a totally objective third-party person to listen to me. I mean, I'd probably get a lot of it out if I just sat and talked to a wall because it just helps to say some things out loud. But to have someone who questions me on things is so helpful. When I say I have survivor's guilt, she asks me why. She asks me where that comes from and what it's about. She really gets right to the heart of things. I think the other thing that has helped me are the support groups. There aren't that many young-adult support groups out there, so I belong to a support group for transplant survivors. Sometimes I talk and sometimes I don't, but just knowing that there are people who have been there and who understand me makes a huge difference. One of the hardest things that people deal with is isolation. You feel like you're the only person in the world going through this, and just knowing that you're not, even though people don't have the answers and can't say the right thing to make it suddenly all go away, just knowing that they've been there makes a huge difference. So I'm a big believer in therapy.

Before I had the Fund, survivorship meant being finished with treatment and having the freedom to live my life independent of the hospital schedule. But now I think it's so much more than that. I started to wonder, when I was diagnosed the second time, if maybe I wasn't a survivor anymore. That was the first thing that I thought. I had gone to the Relay for Life where they had a survivor's lap, an extra lap run by all those who have survived cancer. At that time I had gotten through my Ewing's treatment, but hadn't yet started my treatment for the myelo-dysplasia, and I remember not being sure if I could do the survivor's lap, if I counted as a survivor. But once the Fund came into my life and I started to get more active in young-adult support and that kind of stuff, I started to realize that survivorship means finding a place for all of it in my life. It doesn't necessarily mean starting an organization or being a loud advocate for young adults. It can also mean just reconciling the fact that I've had cancer and fitting it in somewhere. I don't know if it's necessarily *accepting* it, because I don't know if I'll ever accept it, but finding a place for it and growing from it and taking what I can from it are what survivorship is all about. Because at the end of the day, the unchanging fact is, I had cancer.

My name is Sam, I'm twenty-six, and I'm a five-year cancer survivor.

Live strong.

"Even if you're losing, you have to fight."

I became a cancer survivor in 1996, when I was diagnosed with cancer of an unknown primary.

On March 9, 1996, my wife and I were up in New York at a wedding. We'd had a terrific time, and we came home late from New York the next morning and went to sleep. I slept most of the day on Sunday. A friend called, I picked up the phone, and the phone dropped out of my hand without my noticing. The friend said to me, "You sound like you're still tired. Go back to sleep." So I did. My wife had been out, and when she came home I was having trouble focusing on her. My eyes weren't jelling. I went to sleep, went to work the next day, and drove down a street I've driven maybe a hundred thousand times. And the car was veering this way and that. And I thought, "Something's wrong with the car," because I'd never been sick a day in my life. I got into my office and tried to drink a cup of coffee and it fell out of my hand. I tried to pick up a phone and it fell out of my hand. A friend of mine who's a doctor called and said, "Get yourself to an emergency room. You sound like you're having a stroke."

So I drove to the emergency room not believing him. And that's where they discovered that I had cancer. The cancer was in the lymph nodes of my stomach. But they said, "It's not possible that it is an original cancer. It has to have come from somewhere." So they treated me for testicular cancer even though the official diagnosis is cancer of an unknown primary.

I had a terrible diagnosis experience with a specialist from a hospital in New York. I was on a gurney because I couldn't walk. I couldn't see. I couldn't even talk. And this doctor took me to this grand round. A grand round is when all the doctors sit in an amphitheater-like room and look down on the stage. I was wheeled in on a gurney. I couldn't move and they couldn't figure out what was going on with me. They didn't know if it was a stroke. They didn't know what kind of cancer it was. So the doctor came in and talked to them and didn't even look at me. He said, "Case number so-and-so-and-so-and-so. I want you to see what this is." And he took a pronged fork and slid it up and down my foot. And he said, "Could you feel that?" And I said, "Yeah." I mean, I slurred it out, "Yes, of course, I can feel it." And he kept talking to these people as if I wasn't there.

He came around in front of me and I grabbed the microphone out of his hand and said to the audience, "All of you young doctors here in this room understand that I was healthy like you are just three weeks ago, and I hope that you treat your patients differently than this man is treating me." The humanity was missing. Maybe they see so much disease that they forget. That must be what happens. And so I told these kids in there that day, "They ought to give a one-year course in how to take care of patients emotionally and face-to-face. That's important."

When I finished the chemo, I had something called parasthesia, numbness in my feet and at the ends of my hands. That's gone away now. It took a while, but it went away. I was basically off my feet for six months. I'm a relatively active person. I play golf. I go fishing. I take walks. I was also running a business and was used to being on my feet all the time. But when you're off your feet for that long, you really start to atrophy. So I got back into the gym, started working out. But if you want to know the bottom-line truth, I believe getting well is all about mental attitude. That's what I tell the patients I see when

I volunteer. You have to fight. You have to fight as hard as you can. Even if you're losing, you have to fight. Fighting has been important to me. If I hadn't fought at that time, I wouldn't have made it. Statistically I wasn't expected to make it. They told my wife I wasn't going to make it out of that hospital. I wouldn't have seen my three grandchildren. I wouldn't have been doing my volunteer work. I retired so I could spend more time with the grandkids and volunteer. I think it's a wonderful life. It's worth fighting for, no matter what you have. I've heard of so many diseases over these last two years that I've been volunteering, and it's amazing that *any* of us are still here. But you fight anyway.

As a caregiver, my wife was fantastic. She *is* fantastic. But at that point she was phenomenal. She went online and read everything there was to read about the cancer I had. And she took notes every single time we went to the hospital. She wouldn't let me go without her *ever*. And to this day, she doesn't let me go without her. Our friends, these doctors who were in the hospital, said, "You know, she could have a doctor's degree just as easily as we do." She knew as much about what was going on with me as they did. One time she said to me, "Perry, the best-case scenario that I was told when you came into the hospital was that I may be wheeling you around in a wheelchair for the rest of your life, and that once in a while you may be able to get out to go to a restaurant or something." And that's what she had expected. So as far as I'm concerned, the ones who really should be cherished are the caregivers. They put up with an awful lot. They're not sick, but they have to put up with all this sickness. All I had to do was be sick. She had to do everything else. Caregivers need to be recognized as cancer survivors. I believe I owe my life to my wife. I really do. It's not a joke. There wasn't a thing that I couldn't ask her about that she couldn't answer—ever. She's quite a person.

I have no thoughts of the cancer recurring. I may get another kind of cancer, but I don't think the old cancer is going to recur. My wife's family was decimated by cancer. Her mother and her father died from it. Her aunt and a lot of her cousins died from it too. She's the lone survivor in her family. So she's worried about it. But I'm not.

I might be crazy, but I don't believe I'm going to die until I'm ready to die. I wasn't ready to die when I had cancer. We didn't talk about it. My wife didn't even tell me what they told her about me being in a wheelchair until years later. One of my friends out in California came to visit, and he got me on the side, and he said, "Perry, weren't you terrified about the thought of dying?" And truthfully, I said, "No, not at all." At the point that I was when I was so sick where I was recovering from a stroke and recovering from surgery and recovering from the cancer, I was too busy worrying about living, let alone dying. When my friend asked that, it was the first time I even thought about dying.

I had a problem once with guilt of surviving this thing. When I was sick, my nephew was thirty years old and had just gotten married. I think his wife was twenty-eight or twenty-nine. After their honeymoon, she had some kind of cough and was quickly diagnosed with cancer. She died at twenty-nine. He came over to visit me a lot after she died, and I started feeling guilty as to why I, at fifty-seven, did survive, while she, at twenty-nine and just starting out her life, did not. My nephew felt he'd done everything he could for her and said that there was nothing that I should feel guilty about, because he loves me and is very, very happy that I'm here. That made me feel better about it. Other than that bit of survivor's guilt, I'm happy as hell that I am here.

I volunteer every Wednesday to talk to all the cancer patients in the hospital. Every now and then I do feel a little bit of guilt when I see some of the people who are really, really sick, or when I see a very young person who is down with this thing. But when I talk to them, I realize that they're okay. They open up to me faster than they open up to a doctor or a nurse because I've been where they are. I've been through the same or similar treatments. I've been through the whole journey and come out the other side. And they really want to know more. They want to talk about it. It's very good for me, even though it's also good for them. I get an awful lot out of it.

I started volunteering because, while they were so good to me at the hospital and I came out of it so well, when I was there, there wasn't anybody to talk to. I think it's an important thing to have available. I've been through hell with some doctors, who just don't understand how to be human beings. And I think that it is critical that patients are treated by professional people who can talk to them one-on-one.

Before I was sick, I was running a family business with my brother and his son. It's been in the family for seventy-five years. My brother, who's twelve years older than I am, will never retire. Before I got sick I said "I don't want to die in that store." I didn't want to die in that place. So I already had intentions of retiring. When you're tied down to a store, your children graduating from school or playing in a basketball game is not the priority. The priority is staying in the store and watching the business. A light went off in my head and I said, "I gotta be nuts to keep on working like this." So when I got sick at fifty-six, I just didn't go back to work. I sold my part of the business to my brother, worked for another three years, left two years ago, and have not looked back since.

On one of my volunteer trips, there was a woman who had just finished reading a book. "What was it about?" I asked. She said, "It's a story about cancer and surviving." And she said that the thing she got out of the book is that cancer is a word, not a sentence. I think that's a terrific way of thinking about it. You're always afraid of something you don't know. You're always afraid of something you don't understand. But the hospitals and medicine have evolved so much in the eight years since I was there. There are new cancer treatments and new medicines . . . I have full faith that they're going to find something that will really put a stop to cancer. I don't know if it'll be in my lifetime, but it will happen. It's incredible what they're doing.

Survivorship means opportunity. Surviving cancer has given me the chance to do things that I'd never done before. It's given me the chance to talk to people about cancer. It's given me the chance to see my three grandchildren grow up, to not have to work as hard as I used to, to go on trips, or to simply do nothing, which is just as good. These are experiences that, if I hadn't had cancer and I were still working now, couldn't get me out of that store. I've had all kinds of experiences as a survivor. I have survived.

Get out and enjoy your life. Live your life. That's my advice.

My name is Perry. I am sixty-five years old, and I'm an eight-year survivor of cancer of an unknown primary.

Live strong.

"We've got to be part of the solution."

CHRISTOPHER**CARLEY**

I was first diagnosed with what was then called leiomyosar-coma. Since then they have changed the name to just an acro-nym for gastrointestinal stromal tumor. It's a type of sarcoma. That was back in 1996.

The Cliff Notes version of my treatment is that I only had surgery. But really there's so much more to my story. For the type of cancer I have, they can try to extract the tumor, but there is no treatment, no chemo, no radiation, no medication of any sort that is effective in fighting it. So the life expectancy for someone with leiomyosarcoma is, on the average, six months to a year. If it doesn't metastasize, obviously that time can be longer, but it usually does. I had the first surgery for the gastrointestinal tumors that were in my small intestine. They extracted those and said, "We think we got it all." It was great. I was much relieved. But a little less than a year later, it reap-peared. It had metastasized to the liver, which, of course, is a very bad place for it to be. Liver surgery, while it is now still very, very difficult, was nearly impossible at that time. There were only two surgeons in Chicago who would even do the surgery to attempt tumor extraction. Without extraction, there was no cure. It would be fatal. Luckily the surgery was a suc-cess. Again I had no further treatment. But knowing it had metastasized to that point once, I knew it was likely that it was in other places throughout my body on a molecular level. There was a good chance it would come back. So we went very aggressively to other hospitals to get second opinions and learn what the possible alternatives were. We went to Texas for an appointment with the head of the sarcoma group in one medical center. And even he said that there was really nothing he could do for me. You know, my wife and I are sitting there in one of these examining rooms with tears coming down our faces. I said, "Excuse me? Nothing at all?" He said, "No." And I said, "Well, what are my odds?" He said, "Well, about one in a hundred." So we just got up and left. We were devastated at that point. But we got our energy cranked back up, and continued talking to other people and doctors. Finally one of them said that the best thing I could do was build up my immune system as much as I could. He also recommended a macrobiotic diet. It's a fairly stringent diet that eliminates all the bad stuff and focuses on eating the good stuff. That doctor had also said that I had six or nine months to live. But two and a half years later, I was still going. I attribute that to the diet, my improved nutrition, my mind-body connection, a lot of different approaches. Mostly I attribute it to not giving up.

But then it did return. Once again, the only solution was surgery. I went in for what would be my third surgery. They opened me up, and this time the cancer was throughout my abdomen. They said they counted thirty-eight different tumors from the size of a pea to the size of a golf ball. Again there was nothing they could do. They closed me up, and went out to my waiting family and said, "There's nothing that we can do for him." When I came out of anesthesia, still groggy and only half there, I remember the surgeon, who was a very nice guy, saying, "We just couldn't do anything. It was all over your abdomen." I said, "Well, couldn't you have taken some of the larger ones out?" And he said, "It wouldn't make any difference. It's just spreading all over your body." And I said, "Well, what do I have left?" He said, "Oh, it's hard to tell. It could be three months or six months or something like that." And then he said, "But Chris, they're always coming up with new drugs and new cures." And I'm lying there on my back thinking, "Yeah, right. Sure." Well, with the help of some great doctors who got on the case and looked at it on a national level, I found a doctor in Boston. Apparently he was like *the* man on sarcomas. We had tried a lot of different trial drugs before but none had really worked. So we went out to Boston. The doctor said, "Well, there's this really wonderful drug for leukemia on the market." And I said, "But I don't have leukemia." And he continued by saying that if you look at the science, which I didn't quite understand the details of, the cause of my cancer was similar to the cause of this leukemia. Coincidentally they had only found out what caused my cancer about six months before that. I had undergone some genetic testing and sure enough, the cause was a genetic malfunction, a broken chromosome if you will. So six months before, they found out what caused my cancer. Then they found a drug that worked on a similar molecular basis for leukemia. The doctor said, "It's purely theoretical. We don't know if it will work or not." I said, "Bring it on. Let's do it. I don't have any other options right now." The clock was ticking, you know, months, weeks, who knew how much longer I had? But he said that the drug company that created the drug wasn't ready to try it on solid tumors yet. They were just going to stick with leukemia and, depending on their success, they might try it on solid tumors in a year. I said, "A year? I'm not going to be here in a year." And he said, "Well, we'll just have to see what we can do or wait." He said kind of jokingly, "If you know your congressman, call him." So I whip out my cell phone and I call my older brother. My brother has spent his whole life working for the *Wall Street Journal*. And I said to him, "They have this drug. And here's this drug company all the way in Switzerland, blah-blah-blah." And honestly, he marches down the hall to the managing editor, the Number-One guy in the *Wall Street Journal*, and says "My little brother has this cancer and needs this drug . . ." Well, sure enough, a couple of days later, I'm out at the hospital and my doctor comes in. He says, "You won't believe this. The guy that I've been chasing at Novartis for months called me up and said we can start a trial right away." So with a little grace of God, the miracle of medicine, and the *Wall Street Journal* doing its best, a trial came together in six weeks. The doctor said it was the fastest startup of a trial he'd ever seen in his life.

So I was the first person to have the drug for a solid tumor. And it was purely theoretical. When I went on the drug, about half a dozen other people started it as well. We came back about thirty days later from Chicago to Boston and went through all of the tests and screenings. At eleven o'clock at night, my wife and I were in the hotel when the phone rang. And I thought, "Boy, this can't be good news." So I get on the phone and the doctor says, "I'm standing here with a group of seven or eight doctors. We're looking at your scans and we're so excited. Our jaws are on the floor. It's phenomenal. Some of the tumors have stopped growing and others have actually shrunk. It's just amazing." At the time the drug was called STI571. It later became Gleevec and is now an approved drug and one of the first drugs to work at the molecular level going directly to the cancer. At that moment I thought back to that other surgeon, who, not even a year before, had told me that they're always coming up with new drugs. My wife and I hugged and kissed and said, "You know, it's true. These new drugs are continuing to come, and come quickly, and answers are being found all the time." I'm obviously a total believer now. There are answers and they're coming fast. I think we have to have faith and we have to be proactive. We can't be passive. Survivors have to be aggressive. As Lance says, we survivors have to be part of the solution. And I'm trying to take Lance's direction and be part of the solution.

Now I have scans every ninety days to check the status of my cancer, and I'm in great shape. I've had no signs and no growth in the four years that I've been on Gleevec. It's been terrific. A lifesaver, obviously.

I wholeheartedly support clinical trials. When they asked me to be in one unrelated to my specific cancer, the doctors and I knew that it might not be of great benefit to me. My wife and I thought about it. Yes there were some risks, but they weren't great. We immediately said, yes, I would participate, because once again, it's part of this giving back, being part of the solution. So it is very important for patients to pursue trials, not only for their own benefit, but to benefit other survivors and be part of the solution in the fight against cancer. Unfortunately there's a need for many, many more survivors and patients to enlist in these trials. When they don't, it compromises the speed and the effectiveness of the research.

I think diet and nutrition are very important. The philosophy behind the macrobiotic diet that I'm on is basic to many, many diets. I have eliminated the bad stuff: no alcohol, no caffeine, no nicotine. And I eat large amounts of greens and fruits, vegetables, fish, and fish oils. I take vitamins as well. The whole diet is designed to strengthen the immune system. This isn't new news. You talk to any doctor and he'll say you definitely can crank up your immune system by diet. They know that. They know how to do that. So whether it's a macrobiotic diet or some other diet, eating right, exercising and building up your strength all help to fight the disease. As the doctors say, it's anecdotal evidence, but they were giving me months to live, and I went for two-and-a-half years. I really believe that my immune system was cranked up to help me fight the cancer. Everyone knows that when you're depressed or down, your immune system goes down. People who have a loss in their family, or go through something else traumatic, often feel their immune systems weaken. Lo and behold, they come down with a bad cold. And you think, it's kind of adding insult to injury. They were down before and then they get sick on top of it. Well, it's all part of that mind/body connection. So I do believe that doing whatever you can to keep your immune system up, with diet, nutrition, exercise, mind/body awareness, avoiding stress, and keeping the positive attitude, does directly affect your body.

Hope is more important than most people realize. Mental attitude can affect so much. You really have to be positive. You have to have hope. But, I've found, speaking to other cancer survivors, that hope is something that most people don't think about. I remember a cousin of mine who kept telling me, "You have got to get strong to fight this." And I'm sitting there, you know, down, depressed, experiencing side effects from the surgery and the cancer, and I just felt like saying, "You know, I really don't feel like being strong," and, "Gee, I don't feel like fighting it. I'm not in a positive frame of mind." But then I got this feeling of guilt. "Well, gee, I should try to be more positive, you know, to be healthy, but I don't feel positive." It's a catch-22 that I've talked to other survivors about. But you just have to keep moving forward. Follow the cliché, as all clichés are true, of just taking things day by day. Take one day at a time, and try to keep a positive attitude. Be active and pursue solutions. Know that you're working on it and don't give up. Your caregivers and your support group are working with you every day to move forward and find solutions. Remembering all of that will help you to become and remain more positive.

It's terrible when doctors take away hope. Early on I was told that I had one chance out of a hundred, which was devastating. My doctors since then have said that it's a terrible thing for any doctor to do. There should always be hope. Even if it's only one out of a hundred, you should have hope. The doctors who I went to were not only great scientists, but great people who helped me to continue the fight, continue the pursuit, continue looking for answers, and they eventually saved my life. So that positive fight has to be there. My wife and I joke that some days I have a foot mark on my back where she has had to kick me out the door and say, "Okay, let's get going. Quit feeling sorry for yourself." There are bad days, there are terrible days, but then there are good days. The good days will come, and you just have to keep going, knowing that by the grace of God, answers do come up.

I still have some hostility and anger, but not as much as many others, I suppose. Cancer affects different people different ways. There are those who have the banner "why me?" I could never understand that. Why not? Pardon the expression, but I think the more appropriate one is, "shit happens." You can feel sorry for yourself, but that's just not productive. But it does happen. So when you feel down, when you feel sorry for yourself, or you feel angry, you have to say, "Well, I feel this way now, but it'll pass, and I'll get going, or my wife will kick me out the door and keep me going." It is all a part of the process of facing death.

In any crisis, it's automatic to reach out. And reaching out to those who are closest to you, those who love you, is what you should do. Some cancer patients, especially men, and maybe that's my own bias, have a more difficult time reaching out. I'm not sure what it is, vulnerability perhaps. I learned some things when I tried to reach out. I reached out to some close friends, lifelong friends, men who had been close to me all of my life. And I did not get an extended hand from them. It really set me back at first. I said, "Lifelong friend?" And they just said, "I don't want to deal with this, Chris. You know, I'm really sorry, but I can't be there for you." Through talking to other people and getting some professional help, I've learned that it is not uncommon for men to react this way. It's threatening to them to see a close friend about the same age all of a sudden facing death. I wasn't prepared for their reactions, but I did learn the reason behind their behavior. So reaching out is very important even if you can't always expect the helping hand to be there, even from close friends. Try to understand their position and what they're going through. It's very difficult for them. At first I thought, "Well, thanks a lot, lifelong friend. You're not even helping me out." But, you know, it's all part of that human mystery. When facing death you learn a lot more about life and relationships.

Not knowing the clinical earmarks of depression, I didn't recognize that I was depressed. Luckily, my family and my wife did. I think it's part of that male macho thing. You know, "I'm fine. I can handle it." But my family kept at me. Even my children said, "Dad, you need some help." Once my kids were saying it, I had to admit, albeit somewhat reluctantly, that it was a clinical problem that I needed to seek help for. It's not about inner strength or masculinity or courage. It's just part of the human process. The mind is just as much a part of the body as the organs, and it needs care, too.

I often go on fund-raising cancer walks where survivors are very active. We have a great walk in Chicago which the cancer center promotes, called A Walk Along the Lake. Literally thousands of people come out. They all wear the white T-shirts with their cancer survivor group's name. Those who are actually survivors wear purple shirts. I get out there and invite my friends and fellow survivors. And we get out there, and I think it's so great. But when I look around the group, at these thousands of people, there are, without fail, two or three times more women survivors than men. And I'm not sure why that is. I have some theories. But I think more men should be aggressive proponents of fighting cancer. The fight needs all of us. Statistically there are just as many men who have cancer as there are women, and they should be equally active and outspoken. I have to give credit to the women. They are very aggressive proponents of fighting the fight. As a man, I encourage other men to be as aggressive and as outspoken as possible, and to represent survivors for other survivors' sake.

One of the major developments over the past eight years is one that I didn't anticipate. It is my relationship to death. The psychologists have all the different reactions mapped out. There is fear and anger and all these other different emotional stages. I've gone through the stages, but over the long haul, I'm still threatened by death. I go in every ninety days for scans, and that in itself reminds me regularly that I am still threatened with death. My attitude, my acceptance of death has been a very important part of my living. A couple of things have added to it.

During this time, my closest friend, who was my best man at my wedding thirty-eight years ago, was very close to me, and was a friend who definitely put out his hand to support me, at the age of fifty-seven had a stroke. Within three days, he died. All that time, I had been preoccupied and worried about my own death and I lost my best friend. I began to realize that death is something we will all have to deal with. It is a lot. It's scary and it's disappointing but there is a greater appreciation for life that comes from arriving at that understanding.

And then, not even a year ago, my sister came down with a bad cold. I was trying to take care of her. We took her to the hospital, and through a series of tests, within forty-eight hours we found out she had cancer. And here she had spent all these years worrying about me, caring about me, being there for me, and all of a sudden, she has cancer. Six weeks later, she died. It was throughout her body. I think losing one of my two siblings and losing my best friend really brought it home that life is precious for all of us. None of us know when we're going to go. We have to, as they say, live in the moment. Live the day. Yesterday is gone. Tomorrow is not yet here. And yes, we are all going to die. But that's all the more reason to live life to its fullest now. In my professional life, I develop real estate. In these eight years, I have developed almost half a billion dollars in real estate. I have provided jobs and homes for people. I'm very glad as I look back that I did that over the last eight years and that I didn't say, "Oh, I'm only one in a hundred," and just go to bed. I am also involved now in a half-dozen programs, and thanks to Lance, I'm involved in the Lance Armstrong Foundation. I really feel that I'm doing more good in the last eight years of my life than I did in the first fifty. So cancer is not a death sentence. In a way, it's a life sentence that every day from now on is going to be more valuable. I think life has meant more to me, and I have received and given more because I am a cancer survivor.

I met Lance almost two years ago, when he was a young man. In fact, he's the same age as my youngest child. So this young man put his hand on my shoulder and said, "We survivors, we really have an obligation, because of our unique situation, to give back and to fight and to be part of the answer: to be part of the solution to fighting cancer." It just blew me away. I thought, "Here's this young man with his hand on my shoulder hitting me right in the heart with his words. 'We've got to be part of the solution.' " It had such an emotional impact on me and my life hasn't been the same since. He also said of himself, holding his hands up, close together, "This much of my life is about riding a bike." And he drew his hands wide apart, "But the rest of it is about fighting cancer." I still get goose bumps when I think of that. He's just an incredible young man and an inspiration to all of us, even old guys like me.

The real core of being a survivor is continuing to survive. I was given a miracle drug. I want more research, more focus on coming up with more answers for more people. One out of four people will die of cancer. I know it's just a statistic, but it's a big number, and I take it personally. I have four children. I have eight grandchildren. The odds are high that some of them are going to die of cancer. So I see survivorship as an obligation to help find solutions and answers. In the last eight years, there have been so many advances, so many solutions and answers. I'm still here after eight years. And now 98 percent of the men who get testicular cancer are cured. People don't realize the successes. Over 60 percent of the people now with cancer will continue to survive. And twenty years ago, even ten years ago, it was like half of that. So my feeling toward survivorship is, "Let's have more survivors. Let's *be* survivors. Let's do what is necessary." It comes down to dollars and cents for research. Maybe there isn't a silver-bullet cure, but more people are now living with cancer as a chronic disease, like diabetes or heart disease. Let's do things that will allow my children and my grandchildren not to get cancer. So survivorship, to me, is fighting the fight to continue to survive as we all do. With cancer, it's little more hand-to-hand combat, but that's what survivorship is—staying alive.

My name is Chris, and I'm an eight-year sarcoma cancer survivor.

Live strong. It's the only way to go.

"I would not be the Trinika I know today."

TRINIKA**CRAWFORD**

I became a cancer survivor on January 17, 1993, when I was diagnosed with osteogenic sarcoma.

I was a basketball player in eighth grade. I did a running split at practice one day. I hadn't stretched or anything, so when I felt a small pull in the innermost part of my left thigh I was like, "Well, I'm sure it's okay." I ran on it for like two weeks. But then I began to have loss of function in my leg. I couldn't bend it completely. I couldn't run without my leg dragging. And then I had a small bump up on the distal end of my thigh bone. We treated it like a pulled muscle, because that's what we thought it was. I went through therapy with one of our team trainers. That didn't work. It got worse.

So toward the end of 1992, after Christmas, beginning of January, I went to the clinic. I had an X-ray done. And, of course, a big cloud showed up on mine. "What in the world is that?" I said. The doctor determined that it was a tumor and sent me to an orthopedic oncologist at the hospital. He did a biopsy, and that's when I found out I had cancer. I remember him waking me up, shaking me. I was coming out of the biopsy and he said, "The tumor is cancerous." I said, "Okay," and went back to sleep, which is kind of funny to me. I didn't cry at all. I cried when they told me the effects of chemotherapy. The surgeon referred me to an oncologist at the children's hospital.

So I started taking chemo in January. I didn't have the surgery until April of 1993. Before the surgery, the chemotherapy killed 90 percent of the cancer. Then I had the bone transplant, an actual bone transplant, where they cut almost all of my left thigh bone out and replaced it with another bone. I had a plate put in, screws and everything, got a new set of crutches and was well on my way. I continued taking the chemotherapy up until March of 1994. The only complications that I had I caused myself. Yeah, I blame it on myself. I was a track runner and I played basketball, so I was very active and eager to be off the crutches. The doctor said that I'd be on the crutches for six months to a year. So at six months, I stopped using them. I had the original surgery in April of 1993. But then I had another surgery, reconstructive surgery, in October of 1993. And that was because I broke the plate. I put too much weight on it.

I was back on crutches until '97, the year I graduated. I got off the crutches in time for college. I made it the first two years without crutches. But then in 1999, the bone itself broke in half, which was shocking. It broke in half again a year later in 2000. I just got off the cane in November 2002. And now, I am free of cancer and free of crutches. Thank God!

The first time I broke my leg, I was in the kitchen, and I was like, "Momma, my leg feels funny." And she said, "What do you mean?" It didn't feel stable at all. I really can't describe how it felt. I just knew it felt funny. We went to church that night and it got worse. The more I moved, the worse it got. It got to the point where I couldn't even walk. So I was like, "Mom, I can't walk on my leg." She still didn't understand, "What do you mean?" So my brother helped me to the back of the church. We were on our way out. I bent forward a little bit, and when I stood back up, I felt it move out of place. I felt the bone itself kind of fall back to the back of my thigh. It didn't hurt. I just knew I couldn't move. I was like, "Okay, Momma, I think it's broken." So we had to go to the emergency room and go from there to the hospital. My original surgeon did the reconstructive surgery there.

The reason I couldn't feel the break was because of all the subcutaneous tissue, the fat. A bone is well cushioned. It has the muscles around it. And because you have your quads on top and your hamstrings in back, when the bone moves, it falls against the muscle. Even if it's broken, it's really not going to move that much, because it is somewhat contained. So I really didn't feel that much, though I could tell that it was broken.

As of right now, the only lingering physical effect that I have is that I can't do anything too strenuous. I can't run right now. I have not run since 1992, and that's all I used to do. I'm looking forward to the day when I can run again. I've told people that I might be like Forrest Gump. I'll just keeping running. They'll have to make me stop. But that's the only physical problem that I have. I didn't suffer many side effects with the chemo at all. I actually gained weight. I hardly ever got sick even though I had the highest doses of methotrexate and Adriamycin. I didn't feel normal. I had the metallic taste in my mouth, very sore gums, sores in my mouth, that kind of thing. But as far as being nauseated I didn't have it that bad. I was very blessed in the situation.

I would usually go to the hospital on a weekend, on a Friday, to have the chemo. I would miss school on Friday and I'd stay that weekend at the hospital for the chemotherapy treatment. My mom didn't have to work on weekends, either, so that worked out well. I have a younger brother and sister. We're all three years apart, so I was thirteen at the time, my sister was ten, and my brother was seven. They would usually stay with my grandparents on the weekend, because they live right across the street from us. We would come back on a Monday, and I'd usually go to school that Tuesday or Wednesday. I told my mom, "I cannot sit at home. I'm not sick. I can go to school. Just talk to my teachers and allow them to give me the extra time to get to class. I'll be fine." And it was. I went for three weekends straight, and I had three weekends off. And that cycle continued for a year.

Losing my hair was one thing that did not bother me at all, because I'm a tomboy. It was fine with me. I didn't have to deal with it! And when it started growing back, it was really pretty, but I still wouldn't wear it without the bandannas. I loved my bandannas. I wanted nothing to do with a wig. I thought, "If it's not my hair, I don't want it on my head." So I had a bandanna. People used to buy me bandannas all the time. I had a bandanna to match every outfit. And it started a trend at school. A lot of people started wearing bandannas at school because I did.

When you first wake up from the surgery, it's not a nice feeling at all. It's having to go from walking on your own and being very active, to having to walk with aid for six months to a year, maybe more. I was on crutches for four years. Because bone transplants were still kind of new at the time, they didn't know how long one person would be on crutches compared to another. Having to make that transition was the hardest part. I'm an independent person, and having to have people open the doors or carry stuff for me was really frustrating. I told my mom, "There is no way you're giving me a bath. I'm thirteen years old. You can't do that." I wanted to do everything on my own, be independent. And not being able to carry my books, not being able to go out in big, big crowds, because someone could trip over my crutches and cause me to fall, which could cause me to break my bone again, which could cause me to have surgery again, that was rough, especially as a teenager. Having to see all my classmates run around, participate in the sports that I participated in, and not being able to do it myself hurt a couple of times. I had to get over it, but it did hurt.

Meanwhile the crutches kept me in shape. My quads and hamstrings on my right side feel like steel. When you walk on the crutches correctly, not leaning on them, but actually pushing up and using your upper body to get around, you get a great cardiovascular workout. At first, my surgeon, as well as some of my teachers and even some of my classmates, suggested that I use a wheelchair. But I refused to do it. I thought, "I'm young. I can get around on these crutches." I was confident enough with my crutches to walk around on them at the rate of speed that a normal person would walk. I was a pro. I went everywhere. I did everything myself. Even when I was in school, I carried my own books. Walking on the crutches built up my muscular strength and endurance. I also swam. When you're in the water, the body is weightless. It's very therapeutic and helps build up the muscle.

One thing that I can tell a survivor is that the cancer does not define who you are. It's just a part of life. We all have our obstacles. We all have our trials. Unfortunately, cancer was one of mine. But it does not define who you are. If you have goals or things that you want to do, don't stop. Go ahead and do what you can. Just because you are restricted in one area does not mean you're restricted completely. Just because I couldn't walk or run on my own, that did not keep me sitting around in the house. You do what you can. Just don't stop your physical activity. Don't stop living. Set your goals. You may have to modify the way you complete them, but complete them in the best way that you can. Know that you're going to have to put forth some effort, but be realistic about it, too. I knew I had my physical limitations, and I was like, "Okay, this is what I want to do. I'm going to college." I didn't stop. Keep going, but know what your limitations are. Having cancer, of course you're going to be sick. You're going to have your down times. You're not going to feel well. But even when you don't feel well, when you have the metallic taste and sores in your mouth, when you feel nauseated, that kind of thing, make sure you still hang out with your family. Just go lie down in the living room while they laugh around you. Be around happiness. And go into a room that has a lot of color. Or watch cartoons. I love cartoons, because of the color. It brightens the day. Just be around positive things and stay in high spirits. That's what really helps you survive, having that optimism around you; having the drive to want to live and to want to go and to want to do.

I know that it's hard to believe, but I never actually thought I was going to die. My mom asked me one time, "For one moment, did you ever think you were going to die?" And I said, "No." I was always in high spirits, always laughing. And the hospital and Camp Sunshine created that atmosphere for me. And the hospital itself, with the colors and the staff and everything that it offers, helped to promote that positive atmosphere and attitude. It's kind of hard to be depressed when you have so many people surrounding you who support you. Knowing that you have people outside your family who support you just as much as your family does helps out a lot.

If I hadn't had cancer, I know for a fact that I would not be the person that I am now. It is one of the most defining events in my life. I learned a definition of life that I couldn't have learned without cancer. I know that's a crazy thing to say, but it helps you to value life. I actually gained a closer relationship with God. I thought, "Okay. You chose me. I know this is the cross that I have to bear. I know that this probably was written from the beginning. This is one thing that I have to go through." And it helped me to know who I am. It helped me to value life more. It helped me to not sweat the small stuff. And the best part about it was that I was a light to other people without even saying anything to them. Being a survivor and just living and dealing with cancer actually inspired other people to want to live and be more motivated than they had been.

I also wouldn't know myself as well as I do now. I have strength that I did not know I had. If you had asked me when I was twelve, "Do you think you can handle going through cancer?" I probably would have told you no. I had no idea that I could go through it. And I had no idea that it would be easy like it was. A lot of older people would say, "Oh, my God. I

don't see how you do it." And I was like, "Well, I don't either."
I was just made that way and I had no idea. So it helped me to
learn more about me and more about life itself. Of course, I
value and love life more. I appreciate friends and family more.
I appreciate other people more. I met so many people through
cancer. It was also a cultural experience. Now I'm a more
eclectic person. I've come in contact with a lot of different people from a lot of different backgrounds. I'm from south Geor-
gia, so I would not have gotten the exposure to other people
and other things had it not been for cancer, had it not been for
me being affiliated with the hospital and Camp Sunshine. So it
was the most defining event of my life. I would not be the
Trinika I know today if it had not been for cancer.

As a thirteen-year-old girl, you're trying to find out who you
are. The cancer helps to define who you are. You might have
thoughts like, "Okay, I'm ugly. I'm not attractive. I can't dress
this sort of way. I can't look this sort of way. This is not my hair.
I can't try this new style. I can't . . ." The new trends and the
kinds of things other kids and your friends are dealing with, you
sort of think don't apply to you. But they do. As a thirteen-
year-old trying to find out who you are, the cancer will help
you to define the person that you are and actually help you to
deal with those teenage issues. You're going to be more of a
light to other people. You'll actually set a trend for your classmates, instead of you trying to pick up on a trend that's already
in place. Don't be saddened by the fact that you don't look like
the other girls, that you can't have the hairstyles of the other
girls, that you can't do the running around, and you can't go
out all the time like the other girls. Don't be saddened by that.
Be proud of the fact that you have the strength to keep living.
Don't ever forget that you're an inspiration to other people.
Having the cancer and just living with it, being strong and being able to deal with different people, makes you beautiful.
Your beauty is not defined by outward appearance. It's defined
by what you portray to other people from inside.

Survivorship means living with cancer, dealing with it, and going through it. It's knowing that this is what I have to deal with right now. I'm not going to completely stop living. I'm going to continue. Survivorship is really just living. Survivorship is having to adapt to having cancer. It's having the determination to want to keep going.

My name is Trinika Crawford, and I am twenty-four years old. I am a ten-year survivor of osteogenic sarcoma.

Live strong.

"Too sexy for my hair."

CRAIG LUSTIG

I became a cancer survivor on April 27, 1992, when I was diagnosed at the age of twenty-seven with a germ-cell tumor in two locations in my brain.

I initially had surgery to resect one of the tumors followed by a course of three chemotherapy drugs that I received over a six-month period. About a year after I'd finished all of that treatment and had no additional sign of disease, the cancer recurred in a different location in my brain. And after that, I had a high dose of chemotherapy followed by a low dose of radiation therapy.

The physical issues I've had to deal with relate to function that I lost because of the brain cancer. I have no pituitary function, which means that I can't make the hormones that the pituitary gland produces, so I have to take a number of different medications to replace those. Without those, my body can't physically function properly. My thyroid gland doesn't function, my adrenal gland doesn't function, and while I'm physically active, I have certain limitations because of both the medication, which can only replicate what the normal human body does naturally to a certain degree, and my treatment, which gave me some permanent side effects.

In general I can do just about everything that folks with a normal functioning hormonal system can do, but I recognize that I must take my medications at the time that's indicated. If I'm going to be in a stressful situation physically or emotionally, I may need to make changes to the doses of some of them. I work very closely with my endocrinologist, who monitors all of my medications and also the effect of the drugs on my body, making sure that I'm within a normal range on a variety of physical scales. And if he sees any need to change it, we'll tweak the dose. He also gives me advice. For instance, I do some biking, and when I've gone on bike rides for a charity event or something, and it's a longer ride than I would normally do, he'll say to me, "Well, you need to take a little bit more of this." He calls that a stress dose. So it's really about understanding my body and the way it works post-cancer, and not allowing the limitations of my body to limit me too much in what I can do.

After learning that I had lost the function of my pituitary gland and that that would be a permanent effect, I did find people, particularly in the area of endocrinology, who really understood how the pituitary and the other glands that are associated with it function, and they have helped me to turn my cancer into something that, yes, is a chronic disease, but is not something that I feel the burden of every day. I've had to simply integrate the things that I need to do in order to keep my body functioning normally within my lifestyle, and recognize the occasions when I may be pushing myself a little bit too hard and the medication can't compensate.

Something that I don't think I fully realized during my treatment, and something I really try to share with other survivors as they're going through their active treatment experience, is that we all fear chemotherapy. I think it's a word that incites a lot of fear in all of us. But it turned out that, for me, the radiation therapy was more difficult. I had been told that it would probably make me a little tired. But I don't think I have ever felt that level of exhaustion. It was extraordinary. And unfortunately, because I required radiation to both my brain and my spine in order to ensure that there was no additional tumor material left there—no disease remaining after my chemotherapy—I was left with effects and problems in my gastrointestinal system. I think that it's important, when you're going to be having a course of radiation, to understand that for some period of time you're going to feel exhausted. You're going to feel the need to get a lot of extra rest and to really take care of yourself. So prepare yourself for that, and prepare the other people around you so that, if you need to, you can take a little bit of extra time from work or school or your daily activities to rest, to make sure you get the right nutrition, and to really ask those questions in advance of getting your radiation treatment.

Because I received radiation to the spine, it affected my stomach and my intestines. So I had what sounds like kind of a peculiar and silly side effect about six weeks after finishing all of my treatment. I had very, very severe hiccups, what they call "intractable hiccups," which went on, literally, twenty-four hours a day. I had to receive some very, very strong medication for that. The indicated drug is actually an antipsychotic, something they give to people with severe mental disabilities. So it shuts down a lot of your systems, including your muscular system. In addition to stopping the muscular reaction that's happening, it also has an impact on your ability to function emotionally. It was a very scary experience and something that, unfortunately, my caregivers and I were not well prepared for. It happened six weeks after I was done with all the surgery and radiation and chemo, but it was really, in a lot of ways, the worst thing that happened to me. It was very difficult. Anytime I get regular hiccups now, my family and anybody who saw me through that period jokingly say, "He's got hiccups! He's got to go to the hospital!" Thankfully, the bad hiccups have never returned.

It's extremely important, in terms of some of the emotional issues, to have confidence in the treatment you're getting. Believing that you're getting the right treatment and that which is most appropriate for you is very important. I think it's important to go initially to an oncologist or perhaps a surgeon, an expert in your own community, as a starting point. But I do think it's also important to talk to that physician about getting a second opinion. If the doctor says to you that you shouldn't do that, then it's probably the wrong doctor for you to start with. If you have to travel out of your community for a second opinion, go the distance. I think it's incredibly important to get a second opinion, because you need to be comfortable about the treatment decisions that you make. You should be a part of every decision, even though you're not a physician or a cancer researcher yourself. You should, as much as possible, ask questions, talk to your primary-care physician, and really have all the options explored before making a decision about what the appropriate treatment is for you. Take the time to do that.

In my case, even though I was twenty-seven when my brain tumor was identified, after I initially went to a surgeon, it was suggested that I go and see a pediatric oncologist because the tumor type I had was very rare and mostly seen in children and teenagers. So that's where the experts were. Whether the label on the door said "pediatric oncologist" or "adult oncologist," it didn't matter. I just needed to go where the best physicians to treat my cancer were.

I don't think about my hair loss as a long-term effect because I've lived for over ten years with it. After chemotherapy, of course, you lose your hair, and after radiation it's much harder for it to grow back, at least given the location and the amount of radiation that I had. I have tried to grow it back a couple of times over the years, but I've ended up saying, "Ah, the heck with it," because it doesn't grow back terribly well. Now I just shave off what comes up. I was at the airport getting on the plane and the guy taking our boarding passes was also bald or had shaved his head. As I handed him my boarding pass, he said to me, "Oh, you're too sexy for your hair, too." I love that line. I used to tell people that even though I've had these bad experiences from cancer, I think it's so important to laugh about them. If somebody in my family breaks their leg or something, we laugh and say, "Well, at least it's not a brain tumor." It's important to talk about these funny things that happen and the way the world reacts to you after you've changed as a cancer patient. I've had surgeons come up to me in restaurants because they've seen my scar and want to ask about my surgery. It's really peculiar, but I have to laugh and say, "Well, okay." Humor is very important for me as a survivor.

Kids sometimes ask why I'm bald, and I tell them about it. Because I was treated almost entirely in pediatrics, I spent several years among kids and they were a source of great strength and courage to me. So when a kid on the street without cancer asks me about my head, along with telling them that I had cancer and now I'm healthy, I will say to them, "If you ever meet a little child, you know, a friend of yours who may be bald and may look really weird and icky or something like that, be kind to them, because they may have cancer, and hopefully they're going to be okay. It's something that happens." I think losing one's hair is certainly the most outward sign of having cancer. I would think that if you ask a hundred cancer survivors, most of them would tell you that losing their hair was the thing that mattered least to them, but to the rest of the world it seemed to matter most.

Something that all of us, especially young adults, feel at a time when we're coming into our own as individuals, is the loss of control of the body. Having to allow people to do some pretty awful things to it, and losing a lot of control over other parts of your life because you have to devote most of your time to worrying about getting well, is a very difficult experience, and it took me some time to work through that and say, "I'm beyond that, I have control of my life again, and I can once again determine my own destiny." That was a struggle for me. It was also hard working through relationships with friends and family who didn't have cancer but had still been very supportive. Friends in my own peer group found it hard to watch me go through it all. I was somebody who was a young adult like them, but fighting a life-threatening disease. It changed a lot of the relationships that I had with people. I think it's unfortunate that some people have trouble managing their own emotions when a loved one or somebody in their circle of friends has a disease like cancer. But I'm okay with that now. I understand that at times some people need to step back. At the same time, there were other people who I became extraordinarily close to who I had not been close to before, so that was a gift that I wouldn't have had otherwise. I think that my relationships have been something that I've had to take some time to work through and be a little bit angry about but then let go.

I remember that my parents gave me a T-shirt that they had customized and it said CURED or something like that. Then just about a year later I had a recurrence. I immediately ditched that T-shirt. I don't use the word "cured," because I'm not. I will say that my cancer is in remission. I think that I live in day-to-day fear, in part because I did go through a recurrence and I know what that feels like and that it can always happen again. It was a real difficult experience the second time for my family and friends, because I think for them all of the hope of the miracles of modern science went out the window. There was a greater fear that I was going to die. Getting control back that second time showed me that I had really learned a lot about my disease. I did beat it. I beat it twice. That's not to say that the struggle wasn't as difficult the second time around. It was, perhaps, even harder. But I now know that there is life after a first and second bout with cancer.

Survivorship is more than just surviving. It's more than being on the *Survivor* TV show and eating snakes and managing to stay alive. I think that it's about taking your experience and making lemonade out of the lemons. If you got through this difficult time in your life, you should take from it what you can and try to make the most positive experience from it by giving back to others who have cancer or working with other worthy causes.

Survivorship is trying to go forward with a sense of purpose in life and a perspective that isn't driven by fear of disease. Survivorship is being in the place that allows you to go on with the rest of your life and hopefully get even more out of it than you would have prior to cancer.

My name is Craig Lustig, I'm thirty-nine years old, and I'm a brain-tumor survivor.

Live strong.

"Can I sign that thirty-year mortgage?"

MAGNOLIA**CONTRERAS**

I became a survivor in 2002 when I was diagnosed with breast cancer.

I had just arrived home from a business trip. I woke up the next morning with a pain under my arm. I walked into my office and asked a colleague, "What's that myth about having something under your arm? If it hurts, it's not breast cancer, and if it doesn't hurt, it is breast cancer?" And she said, "Oh, I don't listen to those myths. I think you need to go and get it checked." So two days later I called my doctor. They saw me right away. And indeed, there was a lump. That wasn't news to me because obviously I had felt it. The doctor thought it was a reaction to an allergy medication that I was on. "Come back in two weeks." I came back two weeks later. The lump was still there and the doctor was increasingly concerned, because he felt two lumps, not one, this time. So he sent me for a mammogram and a sonogram. I was still not worried at this point because the technician told me that everything was fine, although she still said that I should go see a breast specialist as my doctor recommended. And I said to her, "Well, if you're telling me that I'm fine, I don't feel like I need to do that." And she said, "For your peace of mind, you really should go see him." So I did. They also saw me right away. Next thing I know, he's talking to me about having to do more tests and that it looks like I might have breast cancer. I looked at him like he was crazy and said, "What are you talking about?!" And he said, "It's likely that this test could come back showing that you have breast cancer. I'll let you know Monday morning." So I went skydiving on Sunday, and Monday morning he called and told me that I have breast cancer. I quickly went to his office and said, "Do you know who you're talking to?! Are you sure you have the right patient?" And that was the beginning. Literally hours later, I was under the knife. They did a lumpectomy, and then they started to talk to me about chemotherapy and radiation. All of a sudden, my life was all cancer all the time.

I've always been an obedient patient for my doctors. I have a good sense of who's a good doctor and who isn't. So I felt like I came with some experience. It was easy for me to agree to the treatments and be a compliant patient. My doctor recommended six months of chemotherapy followed by radiation. That I am a woman of color, and that I was only thirty-two at the time, as well as the type and size of the lump, all helped to determine my course of treatment. All of these variables indicated that I should have an aggressive treatment regiment. So I did it all. I had a horrible chemotherapy experience. I lost my hair, lost weight, couldn't eat, couldn't sleep, had hot flashes. I mean, I had the whole kit and caboodle. That was really a difficult experience. That went on for six months, and then I had to have radiation therapy every day for another six to eight weeks. That was horrible, too.

It's been about a year since I finished chemotherapy, which I'm really happy to celebrate. But I think I only started to feel better maybe six weeks ago. I had a lot of lingering symptoms that just wouldn't go away. My body is starting to feel like it used to, but I'm surprised that it's taken so long for me to feel as good again. I worked throughout my treatment. I only took time off when I was very ill with side effects from the chemotherapy. I still work too many hours. I think that physically I'm still in that place where I'll always be checking to make sure that I'm okay. Emotionally, I'm up and down. Some days I feel like I'm having a good day. Some days I feel like I'm having a bad day.

I often find myself reflecting on the fact that I was hit over the head with breast cancer. I had very few risk factors. I didn't smoke, or do any of the traditional things one thinks about in terms of being at risk. So when I think about not having done anything to contribute to having cancer, the idea that now I can do something to prevent it from coming back makes me wonder. I can exercise and eat better and do all those things, but are they really going to make a difference? I'm going through those feelings of, "I didn't do anything to get this the first time. What really can I change to prevent it from happening again?" There's a feeling of a lack of control over its recurrence. If it comes back, it'll come back, because it's just going to do whatever it wants. It makes me angry. I just recently read my very first cancer book cover to cover. And it crystallized for me that now I am a long-term survivor, that this can come back again at any time, that my life before was what it was, but that now I'm in a new phase. This will always be a part of my life. I was initiated into this new world without wanting to be. I'm kind of pissed about it! But I just take it one day at a time and do things to care for myself. I try not to be too hard on myself because every day is a valuable day.

I'm pissed about having to forever worry about my physical health. It's a major factor if I'm thinking about changing jobs. It's an issue if I'm thinking about not working. Health insurance becomes a major concern. It's a primary issue if I want to have children. It's a primary issue if I don't want to have children. So it's this weird variable that's become a primary factor that pushes other things out of the way that I think would be more of a concern for someone my age, like relationships. I feel unique, given my age and being a younger, less-traditional breast-cancer survivor.

As a single woman, I have an incredible level of support; my parents, my family and friends are all there for me. I know that I will always have some level of support. But the level of financial support would become an issue if I ever have to stop working. How would I take care of myself? How would I pay for my medication? How would I just support myself in general? How would I access medical services if I didn't have health insurance? It's like, "Oh, shit. I am completely responsible for my own life and my own care." I'm still young and I feel that life for me at this age is different than it would have been had I not had breast cancer. Before I had cancer, I would go from one job to the next without thinking too much about it. Now I don't feel like I have that level of freedom to be creative and risky about opportunities. I have to be so mindful about having the resources to support myself. I feel like the situation would be a little different if I was older. Breast-cancer survivors are often older women who have families and husbands and who have had time to put some money in the bank. I mean that both literally and figuratively. They have money in the bank but also more support than a thirty-something single woman might have.

One of the things that I did a long time ago, only by coincidence, was get life insurance. I am thankful for the fact that I kept it up, because now I don't have to go through the process of determining whether I'm medically insurable. I'm in. I was diagnosed afterward. So is that some level of comfort? Yes. Had I not had it then, I don't think I would have been able to receive coverage. In terms of health insurance, it becomes important for me to make sure that whatever health-insurance carrier I switch to, whether it's my employer making those changes or my switching jobs, provides the appropriate level of coverage for my needs. I have to make sure that I'm not excluded because of my history, or that they don't perceive me to be in a high-risk group so that my premiums will be higher. It's that level of detail that I'm increasingly mindful of. I'm also trying to take care of myself financially. I'm putting money in the bank so that if I ever have another breast-cancer diagnosis, I know that I can take time off from work. But that raises questions like, Do I buy a house? Do I not buy a house? All those types of issues can certainly affect how I continue to plan for the future. Do I even plan? And for how long of a future? You know, can I sign that thirty-year mortgage?

I am less concerned about the "today" types of things. In talking to other cancer survivors, I've realized that I'm unique in that. I think it's partly because I did really well during my treatments from the standpoint of having support, having friends, and having a good job that worked with me and my illness. Also I'm single, so all I had to do was worry about myself. I didn't have to worry about coming home and cooking or taking care of children or other people. I was completely self-absorbed, and I think that allowed me to focus on getting better and to realize that this didn't have to stop me. It was a huge bump in the road, but it wasn't paralysis. So I think the way that I went through my treatments is part of why I don't feel like this is necessarily going to stop the way I'm living today. But it is having an effect on how I move forward. The future looks very different and the road there is very different for me now than it would have been two years ago. So I can do the day-to-day stuff. What worries me most is what it'll be like in three years or what it'll be like in five years. Obviously, in three years I'll have a better sense of how I'm doing and I won't worry as much about the future. But for now, it's more that long-term anxiety and pressure that I have rather than the day-to-day worries. Day-to-day, I'm doing really, really well.

Because medicine and hospitals weren't new to me before I got cancer, I knew exactly what I needed to have in terms of my medical treatment. I knew what I wanted from my providers. So I was very, very, very careful about choosing my doctors and where I went for treatment. It was important for me to have gone to the institution I went to and to have had the doctor who I had. I think that was absolutely invaluable, because I never worried about getting less than quality health care. That's not to suggest that other people get less care than I did. It was just that it was important to me to feel like I was doing everything I could to get the best care possible. And the way I made that happen was by driving into Boston every day for my radiation treatments. I know that not everyone would have the time and energy to do that. But it was really important to me. It took a lot, obviously. I live about thirty minutes away, forty-five with traffic, but it was something that I needed to do, as opposed to going to my local hospital, where they were not experts on breast cancer. For other people, I would recommend doing the same thing if possible. Find a place where you're comfortable. Find the team that you're comfortable with. That's something that you do have control over. The last thing you want to worry about is the quality of your doctors. I felt taken care of, so I didn't have to worry about every little thing. There were bumps in the road with a provider here and there, but for the most part, I have chosen the group of people who I feel have my best interests in mind for the future. They don't have to be my friends. They are the professionals who I feel will help me decrease my chances of having a recurrence. I feel satisfied that I've done everything I can to ensure that I'm getting the best care possible.

Over time I see my doctor less and less. Now I see him every four months. I'm not sure if I like that though, because I worry that stuff could be happening between visits. At the same time, I'm happy to come in and do what I need to do, get the checkup and know that for another four months I'm doing well. But I can't control what they're going to tell me when I walk into the office. At any point they could tell me that something's going on in my body that I didn't know about. That's the part that is more of a problem. But there's nothing I can do about it, right? All I can do is mentally prepare myself. There is always a possibility that at one of my appointments they will tell me that there's something wrong. I suspect that I will know intuitively before they tell me, but it's still scary.

Every day I see my scars, and at different moments, I can feel them. So I'm never able to completely forget or put it in the back of my mind. The hot flashes are gone now, but they were intense and lasted much too long. I have still a little bit of neuropathy in my toes. I am monitoring my menstrual cycle but not sure if it's going to go back to normal. That's a side effect of all the treatments. Oh, and the chemobrain symptom was a big one for me. Oh, my god! I couldn't remember anything from one moment to the next, and that was really quite difficult. It's better now, but I certainly had intense Alzheimer's moments. And it had a bit of an effect on my work, because sometimes I couldn't express myself. I just couldn't pull out some of the words. But that's gotten better. I had serious hair issues. I was bald, but now it's growing, though it has its own idea of how it wants to come in. Some of these things are obviously more serious than others.

I now have to be much more mindful of when my body's tired. I tend to want to burn the midnight oil, but I can't do that anymore. Now I just go to bed when I feel tired. I listen to my body more. When it feels really heavy, I know that it's time for me to rest, not to go that meeting, and just go home. Over time it's gotten better. I think it's just my body healing itself.

I'm happy that my hormones are coming back, but I haven't had the pleasure yet of putting them into practice. I haven't ventured into many new relationships. I think it's partly due to the self-absorbed focus that you get when fighting for your life. Chemo does something to all of those feelings and emotions that attract you to others and make you feel attractive to others. I think now I'm beginning to feel more interested and invested in relationships and dating and that kind of thing. But I have no idea what it's going to be like to meet somebody for the first time and go through the process of a relationship. When do you talk about the cancer? Before the first date or after? During? I have no idea. If my future is such a concern for me, I can imagine it would be for somebody I might be dating as well. Those questions and answers about my future will have an impact on their life, too. If this person wants to have kids, well, that's not a sure thing with me. And if we do have kids, am I going to live to see them graduate from high school? That's not a sure thing, either. I have a big chunk of a question-mark ahead of me in life but will happily engage in a relationship with someone who can tolerate and help me handle it.

Latino and African-American communities are easily overlooked by the cancer community. For me, it's important to talk to other Latina and black women and tell them to get checked. Go get those mammograms. Do your self-breast exams. You're never too young to begin participating in your avoidance of cancer, in particular, breast cancer. There's a high risk in our communities and it is important for us to make sure that we contribute to being well. So, I'm trying to make sure that people see a dark face and know that they need to do their part in this fight. My sisters need to do their part. The feedback that I've gotten from those communities has been quite positive. People are surprised when I tell them at what age I was diagnosed. People still think that risk factors and risky behavior are really what determines if one is going to be dealing with a cancer. They don't realize that that's the less-likely way to get it. Over 90 percent of the cancers diagnosed are not cause-related or risk-factor-related. And that surprises people. The women who have responded to me have acknowledged what an important message I'm giving them and have appreciated my strength and openness with them.

I have accepted that breast cancer could kill me. I don't think I appreciated that enough while I was going through treatment.

But post-treatment, I have come to terms with death as a possibility. I could get hit by a car tomorrow, but I also know that I could get breast cancer again in four months. And that's more likely to happen than getting hit by the car tomorrow. But over time, I've come to accept that now I am in the survivor club, that I am a member of a club for a disease that doesn't have a cure.

Survivorship doesn't have the same meaning for me as I think it does for other people. I know some people wear it as a badge of honor to convey a sense of, "I've been through something really horrible and I beat it." The survivor part of it hits you over the head, as it did for me. I don't think you have a choice. I think you have to survive. I think you have to make it through, if not for yourself then for people who love you. This notion of it being a badge of honor kind of thing just doesn't resonate for me. For me, it's about being part of this club, a club for those of us with breast cancer, a sisterhood, and knowing that there is no choice but to beat it.

My name is Magnolia, and I'm a breast-cancer survivor.
  Live strong.

"The diagnosis is c—"

DAVID **CARBONE**

I became a cancer survivor in 1999 when I was diagnosed with mediastinal large-cell lymphoma.

My father was a cancer doctor. I grew up in a household where he was dealing with some of the hardest cancer problems of the time. He had gone to work with Dennis Burkett and the Burkett's lymphoma patients in Africa, where one of the first successful treatments for cancer was developed. I saw the pictures he would bring home from Africa of kids with giant tumors that would shrink away with chemotherapy. After coming back to the United States, he helped develop the type of chemotherapy that was used to treat and cure me forty years later. So growing up in the environment of cancer gave me a strange and early background in the disease.

When I was going through school, I was initially more interested in engineering and physics. But that was too dry for me, and I wanted to try to do something more significant with my life, something with people. So I switched to medicine knowing that I wanted to attack the problem of cancer as a career. After practicing for eight years (I got my first faculty position in '91), I was diagnosed in '99. I specialize in one of the hardest-to-cure types of cancer: lung cancer. It's a very common cause of cancer death, very difficult to treat, very frequently fatal. I can still remember the day I got sick. I was out of town at a cancer meeting. While I was shaving, I noticed that my neck veins were sticking out, and I thought, "This is not normal. Something's wrong." Over the next week or two, I noticed a mass in my left supraclavicular area that soon after began to hurt. I needed a chest X-ray. So I had an X-ray, and I saw that I had a mediastinal mass and a lung mass. I thought that I had lung cancer. I arranged to have a CT scan done. I can remember discussing my own CT scan with my colleagues. I put it up on the light box and I said, "This is me. What do you make of this?" I presented my own case at our cancer conference, where I also presented dozens of other patients' stories. It was kind of an out-of-body experience to be saying, "Well, should we do this procedure? That procedure? Figure this out this way or that way?" All along we were talking about me.

We decided on a plan of action. I would have a surgery in two places to try to diagnose exactly what was going on. I was very concerned about cancer at that point, but I hadn't yet been diagnosed. I was originally scheduled for surgery on the day that I was supposed to take my daughter on a field trip, so I postponed the surgery for a week so that I could take her on this trip. Instead I was diagnosed on my son's birthday, May 21, 1999. I had the surgery and they found cancer. At that point, I had to call home and tell them what was going on. They didn't know. I remember very clearly that even though I had worked for ten years with cancer patients, when I called them up and told them I had cancer, the first time the word cancer came out of my mouth, it didn't. I said, "The diagnosis is c—" and I couldn't say it. It was something that just couldn't be applying to me. It was something that in spite of all my training and dealing with this kind of a problem on a daily basis, I just couldn't get out.

So, I started treatment.

I had part of my left lung taken out as well as four rounds of chemotherapy and radiation treatments. I have four kids, and talking with them about having cancer when they were all relatively young was hard. They had a hard time. The girls couldn't really comprehend it. My oldest daughter was nine. But my thirteen-year-old son fully comprehended. He knew what was wrong, and he was very scared that he would lose his dad. And so here I was, forty years old and with four kids, the oldest being thirteen. I was very afraid that they would be left without a dad and without support. My daughters didn't really comprehend it until I started losing my hair. When my hair started falling out, they knew something was very wrong.

My oldest daughter couldn't even look at me. She would look at me and start crying. But when my hair started getting really thin, I came up with an idea. I got my electric razor and I handed it to my seven-year-old and said, "Here, I need you to shave this off." I won't get into the story, but my wife actually left me during this period, too, so I was dealing with cancer and dealing with four children at the same time. I didn't have anybody there to help me shave my head. I thought it would be fun for them. So my daughter took the razor and started shaving, and then my other daughter came up and thought it looked like fun, so then they ended up giggling and having a great time shaving off the rest of my hair. And then my youngest daughter broke out her markers and asked if she could draw a butterfly on my head. And so they drew flowers and butterflies and things up there. They ended up after this episode just giggling and laughing, and I think that helped them accept that there was something wrong but that I was still the same person. My oldest daughter, who couldn't even face it, actually fashioned a wig for me out of corn silk. You know those yellow corn tassels? She's blond with a ponytail, so she made a wig with a blond ponytail out of corn tassels. I have a picture of it that I sometimes use in my lectures. That was also a memorable thing. And it helped bring them into the cancer experience and make them realize that this was not just some stranger that had shown up in their house, but it was their dad, and that I was just dealing with something that changed my appearance. I was the same person inside.

I tell my cancer patients that story and they get a chuckle out of it sometimes. It also helps to be able to tell them the way it feels to lose your hair. You'd be surprised how it can actually be a little bit painful to lose your hair. You walk into buildings with the vents blowing down on your head and it feels terrible, so you have to wear a hat at first until you get used to it. I tell patients these stories, and I think it helps them accept me as their physician. I really understand the kinds of things they go through, having had the chest surgery, having had the one-inch tubes hanging out of my side, having the chemotherapy, having the mucositis, having the nausea, getting radiation, esophagitis, getting all the things that I tell patients about that other doctors can only try to describe: "Oh, yeah, the chest tubes will probably hurt." I can tell patients, "Chest tubes *really* hurt." I can tell them about chemotherapy and how it feels to have chemotherapy. I'm honest with them that it doesn't feel good, but I tell them that I worked every day throughout my whole cancer treatment, except treatment days. Telling patients this seems to give a lot of them some hope that this is not going to totally disable them from life. I encourage them to do the things that they normally do, within the limits of their ability.

I tell my cancer patients that the best way to face cancer is to deal with it one day at a time. What's the best thing to do today? How do I feel today? Have a good relationship with your doctor and develop a plan that's right for you and deal with things one day at a time. They get very worried about what happens when and if this or that part of the treatment doesn't work. And those are all very reasonable concerns. But you have to deal with what you're going to do today. If it's a beautiful day out, go outside and enjoy today. Don't worry about next month or next year. Deal with today. After treatment, it's a little bit of a different story. You go through all these intense treatments and surgeries, and you recover. I found myself at the end of my cancer treatment extremely debilitated. I couldn't walk for ten minutes without being short of breath. There were multiple issues that came up in this post-cancer period. One was appreciating life as I was living it, because I now had proof that I wasn't immortal. Another is that family is an extremely important part of my life and that I need to cherish every day I have with them. I need to continue to enjoy the other people in my life and the things that I do and the interactions I have every single day, because there's no way to know what the next day's going to bring.

I was also determined to take better care of myself. I had been a workaholic. I worked fourteen-hour days and then came home and took care of the kids. Lance Armstrong's image was in my mind through a lot of this, and I was determined to take better care of myself. Ninety-nine was the first year he won the Tour de France, and I had done some cycling. His example is a terrific one. I admired the guy for what he did. So I decided that I owed myself an hour or half an hour a day. I checked myself into a cardiac rehab program. Every single day, I booked an hour on my calendar to go to rehab. I even participated in the Tour of Hope. I did the last day, in Washington, D.C., and I had a great time being part of that finalist group.

People deal with the cancer in many different ways. My ex-wife, when she found out about it, said, "Well, everyone has to die sometime." It was unbelievably cold. She didn't last long. She just left. I was really struggling for a while. I had no one to talk to but my children and my parents, who lived a thousand miles away.

I also found out who my friends were. There are several categories of friends of cancer patients. I kind of played a little bit with putting them into categories. There's the friend who doesn't want to talk about it, pretends like if they don't mention it, that you'll forget you have cancer. And it's well-meaning, but just not the right approach. You're not going to forget that you have cancer just because someone doesn't talk about it. That's one category. Then there's the friend who totally avoids you like you have something contagious that they might catch. And then there are the people who just come out of the woodwork and who, for no apparent reason, do something kind for you that isn't expected. I remember sitting in the first conference when I was in chemotherapy and had had surgery. I was still hurting from having part of my lung taken out, so I was sitting in the back of the conference room, just not feeling very well. And one of the nurses I worked with came up and just kissed me on the cheek, right there in the conference. She said I looked great. I'll never forget that. It was a real kindness that I hadn't expected. And then there was a technician on my hospital floor who had been through breast-cancer treatment. I'd said hello to her when I passed, but I hardly knew her. One day she came into my office and gave me a cap to cover my bald head. "Because," she said, "you can't have enough baseball caps when you're going through cancer treatment." Those are the true friends when you're dealing with this kind of thing. I think it's important for people to know that those kinds of actions mean something to cancer patients. The little kindnesses and the little interactions mean a whole lot and leave lasting impressions. And this avoiding the subject is not a helpful way to interact with a cancer patient. I have finished my cancer treatment and have been able to develop new relationships. I'm actually engaged. So there is life after cancer.

I know it doesn't really sound like it could be true, but I was never really afraid of dying. It's the absolute truth. I've always said, "If I just take it day by day, I will get through this. And if I don't, then that's just the way it was going to be." I was most afraid of leaving my children fatherless. But after I saw that the tumor was shrinking and that things looked good, that became less of a concern. Now, I'm more worried about late side effects. When you have chemotherapy and radiation to your chest, you're prone to premature coronary-artery disease and some kinds of second cancers. But I try not to think about those things too much. Emotionally, I've dealt with this by realizing that in a lot of ways, this experience has really corrected the course of my life. I feel better about myself. I feel confident that

I've dealt with this problem, that I am a stronger person coming out of this than I was going in. I have a very strong relationship with my kids, especially my son. He was old enough to understand what was going on and smart enough to realize what I was going through. I think this experience has bonded me to my children more strongly than before. And so I'm terrifically grateful that this cancer has made me realize the importance of family and strengthened my bond with my parents as well.

Survivorship means having beaten a difficult disease; having greater understanding of what it means to be alive, appreciation for the suffering that other patients have to go through, and a greater drive to improve therapy for future patients through what I do in my job.

My name is David Carbone, and I'm a five-year cancer survivor. Live strong.

"I'm just a regular kid, you know?"

HUGO**GOMEZ**

I was diagnosed with cancer in May of 2000 with a tumor called myxopapillary ependymoma.

I was thirteen when I was diagnosed. I was a football player, and I started having back pain. It was making my life harder and harder. I couldn't walk very much. We all thought it was an injury from football or something. And I had been in a car accident the day after Thanksgiving. My mom and my grandma and me were on our way home from shopping the sales at the mall. We were stopped at a light and were rear-ended by a Suburban. My mom and grandmother were complaining about their necks hurting, but I thought that I was fine, because I didn't feel any pain. But about three weeks later, I started getting pain and it just got worse and worse. I had to quit football. Just walking around at school was unbearable. I started getting pain in one leg and then it started going into the other leg. Soon after that, I was crawling. I couldn't walk anymore. It was really hard going from, you know, running to not being able to walk. My legs were starting to get cold and my parents were getting scared. That's when they took me to get an MRI. The doctors couldn't see anything wrong with me. I went to a chiropractor, and it helped a little bit. But fifteen minutes later, I would feel the pain again. And I just kept telling my mom over and over that I was hurting. My dad started thinking that maybe something more serious was wrong. They took me to the doctor, and the doctor told me that he thought I was making it up. He said that the pieces of the story I was telling him didn't fit together. My mother and I were real upset about that, because I'm over here unable to walk, and he's telling me I'm lying and asking me to jump. After that, we went to a neurologist. When he saw my legs, right away he said, "There's something wrong. Take him to the emergency room." That doctor got everything going. I was in a hospital for two or three days. And I was getting spinal taps and more spinal taps. I got probably around twenty of them, one after another. And I remember that pain. It felt like somebody was stabbing my back with the needle. (What we didn't realize was that they were doing them wrong, causing them to hurt me more than they should.) I remember telling my mom, "I don't want any more." She could tell I was crying. She didn't want them to do it anymore, either, but we needed to find out what was wrong with me. Finally, my pediatrician told my mom that if I was his child, he would send me to the children's hospital in Vegas. So we ended up going there. They looked at the same MRI and found the tumor right away. They gave me another spinal tap, this time the right way with me curled up in a ball so that my spine was opened up instead of lying flat on my stomach the wrong way they had made me do it at the other hospital. And I remember it was less than a day later that I had my first surgery to remove a tumor. After that, I felt so much better, even though they said I would still feel pain for a while. But I got right back up. I got up and started walking. After that, I had radiation for six weeks.

About a year later, I had a relapse. It started at the base of my spine. It was a tumor about a foot long. They compared it to a foot-long hotdog. As fat around as a hotdog and a foot long. They said that they couldn't understand how I was able to walk like that. It's a rare tumor to begin with. That kind usually starts at the brain and moves down. Mine started at the base of the spine and started moving up. So they were trying everything to make it stop, because they didn't want it to get to my brain. So the second time around I ended up getting radiation for about nine months. They had ordered eleven months, but the doctor told me that if we went any longer, my organs would start to shut down, so they stopped at nine months. I had chemo at the same time. And then I had radiation again for another six weeks.

When you have radiation, your skin, where they aim the radiation beams, gets really sensitive. You can't go out in the sun, because it can burn your skin more. And then when I had chemo, I had this stuff on my scalp. I don't know why, but a lot of cancer patients get a kind of fungus, and it grows on your head, because you don't have an immune system to fight it off. So that was really irritating, too. And I had lots of bladder infections and stuff like that. At first, you think you're only going to get the side effects once in a while, but once you start getting them, they just seem to get worse and worse. And then there are all sorts of things with your stomach. The thing about chemo is that it kills off the good and the bad cells. So I went through periods where I was really sick and almost died. I had a blood infection that put me in the ICU for about three days with a 104-degree fever. My temperature just kept going up. But my blood pressure was falling, and they were getting really worried. They didn't know what the outcome would have been if I had waited to go to the ER and stayed at home for another couple of hours. That was real scary. Really scary.

I also couldn't walk for a while. After the second time, I couldn't walk for about a year and a half. I couldn't feel anything like from the waist down. Couldn't feel my legs or anything. I was in a wheelchair. That was real scary. And frustrating because I would see people running and I would just start thinking, "You know, I used to do that." I kind of shut everybody out. I didn't have anybody. My family moved to San Diego in the middle of everything. I didn't have any friends here. My friend Maria came from Arizona to see me. And when she came out, that was like—that feeling was just—I can't explain it. I can't put it into words, you know? I mean, even though she was here like just for a day, it was like a piece of home came to me.

I had to stay in the hospital for about a month and a half after the surgery, focusing on rehab, trying to get my basic motor skills back. It was totally different because I was in a wheelchair. They would teach me how to do things from a sitting position. Learning how to get in bed from a sitting position was really hard. You have no idea how easy it is to get into bed when you have your legs. From a wheelchair, you have to lift yourself up and get to your bed. And if you fall, well, you have to get yourself back up. I mean, you're on the ground, and your bed is three feet high, and some way or another, you have to get up to that bed. It was really hard. They taught me all sorts of things, from how to get onto a curb in a wheelchair to how to get in and out of cars from a wheelchair.

One nurse, a lady named Roxanne, is a big reason why I'm walking. I can't thank her enough. She and my dad are the reason I'm walking. The doctors didn't really tell me that I wouldn't walk again. I mean, the way they put it was, "If you try hard enough, you can do it." But they didn't really tell me, "Oh, you can't walk." I was getting tired of that. I just wanted to know what my chances were from someone's professional point of view. I asked Roxanne. I told her, "Just tell me flat-out, please. I don't want, you know, any beating around the bush. I just want to know." And she told me, "Most people in most cases don't end up walking. After six months, if you're not getting any better, then most likely, you'll stay at this level." Well, when she told me that, it hit me hard. At that moment, I was like, well, maybe this is meant to be. You know? But after playing football and having the mentality of, "No, you can do better than that. Don't just stay at this level. You can always do better," I had some motivation. My mom and dad kept nagging me. But they were really trying to help me. They would get on me, you know, "Don't get comfortable in that chair. You need to try harder." I remember I would get in arguments with them, because I didn't want to try. I didn't want to do anything. I was depressed. And one day, all of a sudden, me and my dad got in this big old argument, and he told me, "I want you to get up now! I want you to get up!" And when I got up with the walker, I just stood there. And he told me, "Let go of your walker." And I let go. And he just froze. I've never seen my dad like that. I mean, he's this big guy, and all of a sudden, he starts crying. It made me think that maybe this was all happening for a reason. And after that, I progressed with my walking. But I'd be at one level, and I would stay there for months. And people would think, oh, he's not going to get any better. All of a sudden, I would jump another level, and I could move my legs, and then I could actually bear my weight. I progressed like that for a long time. After a while, people didn't know what to expect. They didn't know if I was going to stay at that level or not. So all I could do was just keep on trying. It was hard.

Because of the radiation that I got directly on my spine, I haven't grown since I was thirteen. The doctors told me that a lot of patients don't continue to grow after radiation. So I was thinking, "Oh, that's other patients. I'm different. I'm going to grow. Watch." And, nope, I didn't grow. I actually shrunk. But after dealing with it for years, it's no big deal. At least I'm walking and I'm living and I'm healthy now. But I do have to take care of my back. We worry about my back a lot. I can't just be lazy. I've got to be active, because if I start getting pain in my back, then that's bad for me. I've had two back surgeries already, and I'm only nineteen, so I have to be careful.

I have some big scars on my back. People see them, and they'll be like, "Whoa, what's that from?" I tell them and they don't know what to say. A lot of little kids ask, and I just tell them that I had surgery on my back. After that, they want to see it. It's no big deal. I remember when I went to school and I was walking around with a walker and my cane and everything, there were a lot of stories going around. It's shocking the stories the kids come up with. Because I'm Mexican, a lot of people thought, "Oh, he must have been like in a gang or something, you know, because his head is bald." Well, the only reason my head is bald is because I had cancer and my hair wouldn't grow out anymore. I remember another story I heard one time. They were telling me, "Oh, yeah. I heard that you had gotten shot and you were this big gang banger and everything. That's why you were in a wheelchair." I was just like, "No, I had cancer, man." I was like, "I've never been in a gang. I've never done anything like that." And they're like, "What? Are you serious?" I'm like, "Yeah, I'm just a regular kid, you know?" And I remember there were other stories that I'd got in a big old fight and this is what had happened. A lot of people are curious, and they'll stare. And at first, it bothered me. It bothered me a lot. But then I just started thinking, "Maybe they just want to know what happened." That's why people should just ask. I mean, I don't like being stared at, do you?

I would see other kids at the hospital. Like little little kids. Little kids are happy. Even though they're sick, they stay happy. But once you start getting into the teenaged group, it's a lot different. I remember this one kid. He was in a wheelchair. And he was always angry. I could kind of connect with him and understand why he was angry. But then I started really asking him what happened that put him in the wheelchair. And he told me, "When I was little, I was in a car accident, and this is what happened to me." He blamed his mother. He was my roommate for about a month, and I would hear him fighting with his mom and saying a whole lot of things, bad things to her. He was angry at her. He couldn't feel anything from the neck down. I realized that this kid was not going to get any better. Only a miracle would cure him. I would pray for him. I still pray. And it's kind of sad to know that he really can't get any better and I can. I feel kind of guilty about that.

My parents and some of the nurses wanted me to go to a

camp for kids with cancer. I didn't want to go. I was in a wheel-chair and everything, and I didn't really feel like going. But my mom and dad argued with me. They wanted me to go because they knew I was depressed. And I remember when I went to go, I was hoping that I had missed the bus. I was just being stubborn. When I was there, I didn't really talk to anybody, because a lot of the kids were already well. I mean, they had gone through it and everything was over and like okay for them. And me, I was still going through the chemo and everything. I remember this one kid, who became my friend, he came up to me and started talking to me. We talked about music. We liked all the same music and everything. It was cool. I mean, it made me feel better. It made me like feel like I was fitting in. After camp, we would talk on the Internet. Through the camp they have these meetings once a month, and all the cancer patients come and see each other. And the parents have their meeting, and they can all talk about what they went through or what they're going through. The siblings, they have their own meeting, too. They can just make each other feel better by talking about what they've experienced. Anyway, one month I was supposed to go to the meeting this one last time, and for some reason, I just wanted to stay home. I didn't go. And about two weeks later, I found out that my friend from camp had passed away. When I heard that, it was like, "What am I supposed to do now?" My friend who I thought was going to live when I thought I was going to die, just passed away. I went to his funeral, and it was just . . . I saw the pictures from his last days and everything. I saw him at camp and he never looked like that. I mean, this kid was always happy. He always smiled. I remember that about him. Even when things were going wrong for him, he would always smile. And I remember I'd always be grouchy, always grumpy. To see a good person like that pass away was just really hard. Really, really hard.

There was a point when my mom and dad wanted me to go see a counselor. I didn't want to. I'd actually argued with them not to go, because I didn't think I needed to go. It's hard to go

to a counselor and have him say, "You know what? He really
does have depression." It's more hurtful for somebody else to
say that about you than for you to say it yourself. I knew it, but
I was like, "I'll deal with it. It's okay." I would break down a lot
of times. I'd break down and cry. I would only cry when everybody was in their rooms and I was alone, but I was really hurting inside. It was hard to deal with, but I had faith in the Lord
and in my family. All you have is your family and your faith.

At first I was really angry toward God. I mean, you don't expect something like this to happen to you. It just hits you out
of nowhere. And I was angry at God because I was thinking,
"Why me? Why my family?" But my mom always said, "You
can't think that way. You just need to pray." After a year and a
half of just being mad, I started praying, and it made me feel
better. I would fight with my parents a lot, because I was angry,
because I didn't want to be in a wheelchair. I would have rather
died. At least that's what I was thinking. I went from walking,
running, and playing sports to being in a wheelchair. You don't
want to be that way. I mean, it'd almost be easier to be born that
way, because then you wouldn't know the difference. But once
you have had it and it's taken away, it just hurts. Then one day
I kind of snapped out of my depression. I was like, you know,
I can't live like this. I'm slowly dying. It was bad enough that I
was dying from the chemo, but I was basically killing myself
with the depression. And after that I realized that I needed my
faith. So I just prayed. I would pray and I would pray. My faith
got me through.

I've had a girlfriend for about two years now. She's a great person. When I met her, I was still in the wheelchair, and she was
a cheerleader. I thought, "She probably has a boyfriend. She's
not going to want to go out with me." So I didn't really bother
to ask. I met her because of my mom. My mom wanted me to
get out and meet people. And there was this lady who worked
for my mom and she had a daughter. They had gone through a
whole bunch of things, too, because her brother had died. We

went to watch a Raiders game on TV with a bunch of people. I love the Raiders. And I met her there. I didn't try to talk to her. I just kind of . . . I just liked her too much, and I was kind of shy. But we started talking. And I just talked to her for I would say about a month. After a while, I asked her out. And that's when everything started changing. I was happy before, but it was just kind of a content happy. But it's different when you have somebody your own age to talk to, someone who is not family. I met her and it was totally different. She helped me a lot.

I live strong by living every day as if it was my last day. I thank God that I'm here to wake up in the morning, to go to sleep at night, and to do the things that I do.

My name is Hugo Gomez, I'm nineteen, I'm a four-year cancer survivor and I live strong.

"Pity? Move it along."

SUZETTE**GELLE**

I became a cancer survivor on April 18, 2002, when I was diagnosed with ovarian cancer.

It's been a roller-coaster ride, lots of good, not all bad. Lots of doctor visits. But life all in all hasn't changed much. It's still good. I still do all the things I want to do. I think my life changed more mentally and spiritually than it did physically.

I learned to be a self-advocate right from the beginning with my primary doctor. The story still scares me to this day. Back in February of 2002, I made a doctor's appointment. The month before, I had some terrible pain at work one day. It was so bad that I couldn't stand up. I was totally bent over. Of course I didn't want to draw attention to myself, so nobody knew except the person next to me. She heated up my lunch for me and I said, "Please don't tell anybody." I just sort of waited it out until I could stand and go home. I went to my doctor two days later. I didn't know what was going on. I thought that maybe I had appendicitis. A hernia? I had no idea. He did his exam. He was pushing on the area. I almost kicked him, it was hurting so bad. My knee jerked up. And then at the end of the exam I said to him, "Should we take a picture of this?" And he said, "No, I don't think so." "But it's pretty bad pain," I said. And he kept insisting that I didn't need an ultrasound. So I let it go. He said, "Come back in a week if things are still hurting." I went back two weeks later, because I had started to bloat up. My abdomen started to fill up. I could feel that my clothes were tight. I just felt that so many things were not right with my body. I went in and he goes, "Oh, women your age, you know, you gain weight." I said, "No, no, no. You don't gain sixteen pounds in two weeks. No. Even if I ate twenty-four hours a day, I'm not sure I could gain sixteen pounds in two weeks. Can we take an ultrasound now?" "Uh, no, I don't think we need to. You know, women your age . . ." he went on and on. So I let it go one more time. Then another week went by. It was getting more uncomfortable. I left a message with the doctor saying, "If you don't give me a referral for an ultrasound when I come in on Tuesday, I will be going to the emergency room. And I am going to blame you for not giving me a referral." Of course, I walked in and he had the referral. That was the start of advocating for myself. I felt a little weird about getting a second opinion, like I was cheating on my doctor, because I really did like him a lot. But I did it anyway. I had to.

Because I had ovarian cancer, I had to have a full hysterectomy. At the time, I was just worried about saving my life so I wasn't worried about losing my "female parts." I was forty-five years old, so not having kids wasn't as big a deal as it would have been if I was thirty-five or twenty-five and in the same situation. At the time, the only thing I could focus on was getting the cancer out of there so I could live. After the surgery was done, my self-esteem didn't go down, but boy, my body image sure was different. I didn't know if I'd ever look the same. Everything looked a little bit out of whack, because, you know, they cut me down the middle and stapled me back together. I thought I was going to lose my belly button, but my surgeon did a wonderful job. Today you can hardly tell I even had surgery. I look at my scar sometimes even now and I think, "I can hardly believe what happened there." But the first time I looked at myself in the shower, I was like, "Oh, my god!" But as things physically started getting back to normal, my body image got back to normal, too. I don't think too much about it anymore. You take whatever you have to take. I didn't want to lose my life yet.

I asked my surgeon about my prognosis and how he thought I would fare in the future. You know, let's be honest. I asked him how long he thought I might live. And he says, "I won't get into that. You're a statistic of one. We don't talk about that." (The stats for ovarian are not very friendly.) Maybe they don't talk much about the long-term because they don't want you thinking about it, dwelling on it. But I know every time I go for a treatment that there's going to be some kind of damage down the line. You know, somewhere down the line something's getting lost, whether it be healthy tissue or bone density. I'm going to enjoy what I've got right now and not worry about down the line. If I have to deal with the long-term and deal with a secondary cancer, I'll just be happy to be here that long to get a long-term effect. I try not to think about it too much. I want to keep living and loving what I'm doing right now.

Physically, the worst part during treatment was losing my hair. That was the hardest part because I felt that my secret was out. Everyone pretty much knows you're facing some kind of cancer once you lose your hair. And then it's just a matter of when they're going to ask you about it. But up until the point you lose your hair, it can all be hidden. Even though I was often fatigued and sick every three weeks, I was able to hide it from people. At work, not everyone knew why I had been gone for five weeks until my hair started to fall out. At first I didn't want them to, but they all sort of rallied around me in a very positive way. It was a "You know you can do it!"-type deal. That I could handle. But I couldn't take the, "Ohh." The, "Oh, I'm so sorry." That I couldn't handle. It made me feel pitiful. I did have a couple of people approach me, but they ended up being good experiences. I realized they were only asking because they cared and because in some cases they had been through it themselves. My initial reaction was always tension and anger, but they would always say right away, "I'm only asking because I've been there." And then they would share their story with me, and it became a good experience.

The bad part mentally is that you're facing your own death, which I wasn't ready to do at forty-five years old. I wasn't prepared to think about it yet. Of course, we all know we're all going to go eventually, but cancer forces you to face the reality. That's the worst part, just trying to deal with the fact that life could end earlier than it should. That can turn to anger. It can turn to pity. "Oh, woe is me," you know. I've gone through all of those reactions but have managed to get out of them, too.

I'm deathly afraid of pity. I don't want people feeling sorry for me. At home, that was my biggest problem. The people I live with were getting sad about my being sick. And I didn't feel that my life was pitiful or sad. I didn't want anybody saying to me, "Oh, it's so sad." No, it's not. It's just something that happened. It's sad, but then it's not sad. I didn't want to hear it. And I didn't want a lot of pity from strangers, either. That's why I wanted to keep everything a secret.

I said to my family, "If you're going to be like that, you've got to go. We won't be able to do things together, because I can't handle people feeling sorry for me." It's a hard thing to say to people you live in the same house with, but if they're going to come around every time they see me and go, "Whoa," you know, it's just not going to work for me. I don't feel that way, and I'm the one who has the cancer! If they're going to cry, they're going to have to take it somewhere else. They should go find a support group, do whatever they need to do, because I can't be around that. I just want to be treated the same as I was before the diagnosis.

Pity makes me angry because I feel that my life is great. I like myself and I have good self-esteem. And I don't want anyone thinking that my life is less than what it was before because of cancer. That's ridiculous. I mean, if you're going to feel pity for me, number one, pick another reason, and number two, keep it to yourself because I don't pity myself, so I don't want any from anybody else. It's wasted emotion as far as I'm concerned. You want to toss me something, toss me some encouragement, some love, some kindness, TLC, whatever you want to call it. But pity? Move it along. I've got no time for that. That was why pity was my biggest fear.

I joined a support group in Philadelphia. I needed it. I reached out right away. As soon as my surgery was over and I was able to get around, I called my doctor. He recommended that I go there, so I did. It was a room full of people who were just like me, who were facing the same fears that I was. They were facing death and the realities of maybe not being here as long as they thought they were going to be. It was a big help in learning how to let go of the anger, though that just sort of has to come on its own. Sometimes I still feel it. Sometimes I still have the anger and sometimes I still mourn for my old self. I can still remember myself from three years ago before all this happened just by looking at a photograph. I'll see myself in a picture and go, "That girl didn't know she had cancer."

Those kinds of feelings just sort of wound down on their own. I'm getting ready to graduate from the support group, because it's been almost two years now and I want to do more with my story than just sit in a room with five people. I want to get out there and advocate and try to show people that life can still be great. I still love life. I still do, even on a bad day, because even people without cancer have bad days. They get depressed. They get angry. You know, it might not be about death per se, but they still get angry, they still get sad some days. So I just want people to see that life can still be really great. I'm so glad I'm still here. I just want to share that with everyone and maybe help some other people get over those humps a little bit easier than I did.

I've noticed some cognitive changes, side effects that do not make me very happy. I feel my memory is gone a little. Not totally gone, but it's worse than it was. When someone asks me a question, I might forget it, honest to God, fifteen seconds later, which can be embarrassing. I know it shouldn't be that way. I'll be talking to someone and then all of a sudden say, "Could you repeat that? What did you just say?" Trying to concentrate for a long time is difficult, too. Like reading, for example, I can only read for so long before the concentration starts to go and I have to stop.

They say that leaving Post-it Notes everywhere helps with the memory thing. I've started doing that. I've been leaving them everywhere that I pass in the morning on my way to work. You know, I'll stick it right on the bathroom mirror, on the door, on the calendar, anywhere that I know I'm going to look the next day . . . in my wallet. I also have this memory game on my computer that I play to try to improve my memory. I try to play it every day. I've had this game for years on my computer, and now I use it every day in the hopes that it's strengthening any weak cells that are up there. It also takes me a little longer to get things done at work than it used to. I work with a guy who I had to make repeat stuff an awful lot. But not anymore, because now when he says anything, I'll say, "Wait a second, let me get my tablet," and I write it all down. That way I don't have to keep asking him to remind me of things. Everybody at work has been so supportive. I've actually seen other people using Post-it Notes who didn't use them before. So you know, maybe I'm spreading a good thing around the office.

I've had some issues with my immune system being compromised. In my first go-round with treatment, my white cells were hit pretty hard, to the point where I needed booster shots of a drug called Neulasta. And that just added to what I was already getting with the treatment, because it caused more muscle pain. There are a few more aggravations with the drug, but you know what? Taking it is better than getting a cold and landing in the hospital because of it. I think I needed two shots out of six rounds of treatment last year. Since then, I've had a slight relapse. Now they're giving me Procrit, because the red cells are the ones going down, not the white. So when my white cells go down, I can't lie, I get very nervous about being around anybody sick, about going outside too much, going to any parties, even being at work. If anybody around me is sick, I'm like, "Oh, don't hand me that," or, "Can you just touch it with your fingertips? I'm sorry to be annoying, but my white cells are down." I just sort of announce it. And so far, knock on wood, I haven't gotten sick at work. I've been around a lot of sick people. I can't believe here I am with cancer, on treatment, and I haven't gotten as sick as the "healthy" people around me. I don't know if it's the shots I'm getting or the flu shot or all my vitamins. Anyway, something's working.

After treatment, I ended up with some pain. I had taken all of my chemo in my left arm without a port (which people in my support group think is very hysterical, because everyone should have a port). So I took it all in my arm, which really messed up the veins. Midway to two-thirds of the way through treatment, my shoulder really started to hurt. It was getting on my nerves until somebody in my support group popped in and said that he went to a massage therapist. So I asked for the name of the guy. I go to him now and the pain is gone. I don't know whether I attribute it all to him, or to him and vitamins and exercise and everything else, but it's gone. I'm starting to feel a little pain on the right side now because this time, with the small relapse, I'm taking the chemo in the right arm. But I've told my massage guy about it and we're going to start making it go away, too.

Neuropathy is also something I'm dealing with. I think it's a result of the drugs that are in my chemo cocktail. It feels like a tingling in my fingers and toes. During treatment, I had it really bad. It went beyond tingling. It was actually painful. My toes hurt for days after treatment, and I would say the tingling kept up for a good few months. Six to eight months after treatment was over, I was still feeling it. It got to the point in my fingers where I couldn't even shut off my clock radio because I couldn't tell if I was touching it. But all of that is okay now. The feeling is back. Unless it's too cold outside, I feel okay. The thing about neuropathy that's so terrible is that there's really nothing to do about it. Whether the massage helped that, too, I'm not sure, but I'm not feeling it anymore. And I do know of other ovarian-cancer patients who are still dealing with it today. I guess I'm one of the lucky ones, because I feel totally fine with it now.

After getting a cancer diagnosis, your outlook on life changes immediately. I would say for the most part it's a good change because now I really love every minute of this life. Before the cancer, I'm not sure I loved it the way I do now. Now I want to do as much as I can. I'm going up in a hot-air balloon ride next year. And I know that's coming from the cancer diagnosis, because I was going to wait and do that when I was older. But I thought, "You know what? I'm going to do it now." I enjoy life more now. I live more for the moment now than I ever had before. Cancer stinks, but it doesn't ruin your life. You can have all the fun you did before, and if you're lucky enough to get all the support that I have gotten, it makes life even better. I appreciate everything I have so much more.

I consider myself a very hopeful cancer survivor, because I always look to the future. I look to the future as if I'm going to be around for a long, long while. Sometimes I worry that I might not, but my hope is that I will be. The medical community calls ovarian cancer a chronic disease now. It's something that could go on endlessly throughout my years here. It took me a long time to get used to the word "chronic." When I was at a seminar I heard it for the first time. One woman said, "chronic" and one doctor and I actually went, "Ouch!" you know, like really loudly. People laughed. I just couldn't believe she said that. And she said, "But 'chronic' is a good thing." It took me a while to see what she meant. But yeah, it is a good thing, because it means you're going to be here a little longer. You know, if it wasn't called "chronic," they would just tell you,

"Start getting your affairs in order. Because you won't be here tomorrow." But chronic means you're going to be here a while to get tortured, which is okay. It's A-okay. Bring it on.

So I'm hopeful that I'll be here long enough to see them coming out with new stuff that could keep me here even longer and with fewer physical side effects. For example, with the drug I'm on now, I still have my hair. And just ten years ago, that drug wasn't here. I'm hopeful, because I want to be around here long enough that they'll have something new and better. I want to be here to try it should I have another relapse.

So I'm hopeful that there will always be something new. I try to read every article on ovarian cancer that I can get ahold of. I know what's new and what's coming down the line. For example, I know that the drug that I'm on now, by next year, should be available in pill form instead of just in an IV drip. I won't be sitting there in the hospital for a half-hour with a needle in my arm. So I have lots of hope. I want all cancer survivors to have hope, because there's always something new out there for every kind of cancer. There will always be something new.

Uncertainty is not always a good issue for me. It can cause a lot of anger. I'm not certain that I'm going to make it to an old age. You know, I look at my credit card and I see the expiration date, and I wonder if I'm going to expire before my credit card does. And that bugs me and makes me angry that I might miss out on some time here. But I'm trying to cope with it. I often get jealous of people who still sort of have their illusion of living forever. Because we're not going to. None of us are. And those of us with cancer or other illnesses know for sure that we're not. For me it's right there every day. The good thing is that it makes you live more for the moment, for today, for this minute, and not think about things years from now. Just live for right now.

To me, survivorship means having enough strength to go on when things aren't looking that good. It means wanting to fight to keep living even when the situation is dire. It means getting stronger each day with thoughts that you can keep going, even if you hear things you don't want to hear, like "chronic" and "relapse." It means that you are strong enough to go on and keep loving life. That's a survivor. I will not give in until the last breath is out of me. I am going to be fighting to the very end.

My name is Suzette, I'm forty-five years old, and I'm a one-and-a-half-year ovarian cancer survivor.

Live strong.

"I felt I had gotten off too easy."

TIM**MADDEN**

I became a survivor when I was diagnosed with testicular cancer.

I was diagnosed in November of '99 and I had an orchiectomy a couple of days later. I was originally treated in Boston but was working in New York, so I was sent down to a hospital there. After the surgery, we just watched things to make sure nothing had spread. I had three pathology reports. And two of them read that there was vascular invasion within the tumor, meaning that there was a chance that the cancer would have traveled somewhere else. The doctors at the first hospital said that it was a low enough risk to just watch it. But when I got down to New York, they were fairly aggressive. They wanted to give me a lymph-node dissection. And so I decided, being twenty-five years old, that I wanted to be as aggressive with my treatment as I could. I was kind of fired up to have the surgery done. In January of 2000, I had the lymph-node dissection. One of the risks of the surgery is a 10 percent chance at loss of ejaculatory function or retrograde ejaculation. As it turns out, that happened to me. So that's one of the things that I now have to deal with going forward.

The way I discovered I had cancer was interesting. My left testicle was the one with the tumor. It was getting really, really big, but had grown so gradually that it wasn't like I woke up one day and it was swollen. But it was just getting bigger and bigger. One night I had a couple drinks with my buddies and I said, "Dude, check out the size of my nuts. I just have really big nuts." And they were like, "Bro, there's something weird going on there." But like I said, it was so gradual that I didn't see it as a problem. Then one night I was having dinner with my dad (I have a great relationship with my dad), and I was sitting there after a couple of glasses of wine. I said, "Pop, check this out." And he goes, "Tomorrow you're getting that checked out." So I went into a hospital in New York City, and I first saw my primary-care guy. He took one look at it and said, "I want to do a chest X-ray." He did a chest X-ray and it was clear. Then he said, "I want you to see a urologist. I think it might be a tumor in there. We need to be sure." So I went to this eighty-two-year-old urologist. I sit down in front of him, and he starts talking to me. And he says, "Listen. I'm sure it's nothing. But we need to kind of check it out." I said, "Fine. That's great. I'm glad you say it's nothing. That's a relief." So we go into the exam room across the hall from his office. He has me strip down naked, and he puts me on the exam table and looks at me. "Yeah," he says, "I'm pretty sure this is fluid. But hold on one second." And he's looking up in the cabinets. He's clearly looking for something he can't find. He says, "I'll be right back," and he opens the door and goes across the hall, leaving the door wide open. Nurses and patients are walking by and I'm buck naked. I'm 165 pounds of naked sitting on the table. And I'm incredulous. He comes back in, turns out the lights and closes the door. He's got a flashlight. And now my fists are clenched. I don't know what this guy's going to be doing to me. I started getting really weirded out. He didn't say anything. He just comes up with the flashlight. What he was trying to do was see if there was a solid mass there through the flashlight. He says, "It's just fluid." He turns on the lights, "But just to be sure, we're going to send you down for a sonogram." I went down and got a sonogram. And the technician immediately went out and grabbed a radiologist. They're gelling my left testicle and using the sonogram, and she's looking at it and they're talking to each other. And I just turned around and said, "Well, what's going on here?" And she says, "Well, there's something here." And I said, "Well, do you mind telling me what it is?" She said, "Well, there's a solid mass." I think I actually said, "What the fuck does that mean?" And she said, "There's a tumor in your left testicle." I said, "Okay. Print all that up." She said, "Well, I'm going to send it up to the doctor." I said, "No, don't send it up to the doctor. Just give it to me." So I physically took all of those slides and everything from the sonogram, went up to the doctor, shook his hand, and said, "Looks like it's not fluid." He says, "Well, we should talk about this, and, you know, get you into surgery in the next couple of days and take it out." I said, "Would you be doing it?" And he goes, "Yeah, it's a pretty easy procedure. I'll take care of it." I said, "Yeah. I really appreciate your help, but I'm out of here." And I called my dad's friend who is a doctor in Boston. He hooked me up with a urologist who took it out a couple of days later.

When I was going through my diagnosis and treatment, a lot of people got kind of scared. I had a lot of support from family and friends, but every once in a while, a buddy of mine would just be scared and not know what to say. I'd try to help them out by saying, "There's nothing to say. Just hang out and talk to me. Ask me questions." My way of dealing with it was to be very open. And I think that that's helped me to deal with going forward. I'll be the first one to break out my scars for anybody who wants to see them.

Even when I've been dating, I've always been open about having had cancer. If I go on a first date, usually within the first half-hour, they know that I've got one testicle, they know that I've had cancer, and so on. I think, number one, it's a great conversation starter, and number two, it is something that makes me who I am, so they should know that before going in.

The reactions have been mixed. I think most people are kind

of like, "Wow. You're so open about it." Or they say, "Oh, my God, I'm sorry." Some people don't want to talk about it, while others want to ask questions, to which I'll say, "Honestly, if there's anything you want to know, whatever it might be, please ask." So it's a mixed reaction, but usually it's a good one.

After the surgery, everything seemed to be going pretty well. There was no cancer in my lymph nodes. I continued to get regular CAT scans and other monitoring tests until about a year later, when they noticed that there were enlarged lymph nodes in my abdomen. Over the course of three weeks, they decided that they wanted to go in and do a biopsy. Thankfully, the biopsy turned out to be negative. Around the same time, my mother was diagnosed with lung cancer, so I moved up to Boston to take care of her and be closer to her. She passed away a year and a half ago from the lung cancer.

Meanwhile, everything seemed to be pretty good with my scans, my checkups, and my blood work. Everything was good up until last November, which was about four and a half years after the original diagnosis. I had gone in for a CAT scan. And when the results of the scan came in, the doctor said that my abdomen was fine, because the lymph nodes we had biopsied before had kind of stabilized at their enlarged size. He said, "Your abdomen looks fine, but there's a bunch of stuff in your chest that we're kind of concerned about." So he ordered a PET scan to see exactly what we're dealing with. The doctor was fairly certain that the testicular cancer had come back. I went in for the PET scan and my chest lit up like a Christmas tree. They went in and did a biopsy of some lymph nodes in between my lungs. When they removed those, they turned out to be sarcoid. So it was all benign, no cancer, which was obviously a relief. But there was a good month and a half when I didn't know what I might be dealing with. I thought that it was all coming back and that I was going to have to deal with chemo. I originally never had to go through chemo. I got lucky. But I started preparing myself for it. What I didn't realize while

I was worrying for those six weeks was that the doctor was in-
experienced in recognizing that this wasn't a recurrence of the
testicular cancer. I ended up going back to Boston, where I was
originally seen, and I saw the doctor there, and he said, "I never
would have told you that your testicular cancer had come
back." He said, "You're just too far out. There was a chance that
it may have been something. You know, it could have been a
lymphoma or something else. But there was also a very good
chance that it was sarcoid. I would have told you that originally." I felt that I had been put through six weeks of craziness
for nothing. I was lucky, though. And so far, that's been pretty
much it. Now I'm seen once a year and when I get a clean scan,
I'm good to go.

I definitely have some physical side effects. I have some scars,
which I don't really have a problem with. I've only got one testicle. And then there's the retrograde ejaculation, which happened because of the lymph-node dissection. That's probably
the biggest thing. I'm not married yet. I'm still single. I did
bank some sperm before any of my original treatment. That
was an interesting experience in and of itself. You know, you
go into this hospital room and the nurse gives you the cup, and
you go in and you do it. And I think I did it about seven times.
It was actually kind of funny, because when I was going to do
it, my mother said to me, "Oh, sweeties, I'll drive you over
there." I was like, "No, no, no, no. Listen, Mom, I'm taking the
train." The last thing I wanted to do was get out of the car, give
my mom a kiss, and go in to do what I had to do. "No thanks,
Mom. I'll take the T. I need to think about some stuff before I
get there." It was kind of a comedy. Other than that, my physical side effects have been pretty minimal.

You know, I never really got mad about having cancer. Never
got mad. I never said, "Why me?" A lot of people ask me, if I
could, would I take it back? Would I not have had that operation that made me lose my ejaculatory function? And my

answer's always been that I wouldn't change a thing. I wouldn't change the fact that I had cancer. You know, the fact that I have had cancer makes me who I am today. I think it really gave me more of a sensitivity to other things. When my mother was dealing with her cancer, we had a weird special bond. Before her first CAT scan, I told her what it would be like and what to expect. And now, when I'm at a hospital, or just anywhere for that matter, I feel very comfortable talking to anyone who has been diagnosed. "Hey, you know, it sucks, but you're going to be able to deal and you'll get through it," or what have you. I've always felt extremely lucky. I go into the hospital to get treatment or I go in to get a CAT scan and I see a six-year-old boy who is run down, totally bald, going through chemo, but with this huge smile on his face. So when I see that, I think to myself that I had it very easy. Some people don't really understand that. They don't understand that I didn't have to have chemo. You know, testicular cancer has a very high cure rate. Yeah, I went through some surgeries, I went through some interesting times and stuff like that, and I've dealt with some stuff going forward with regard to guilt and the retrograde ejaculation and so on, but I've never been mad. Guilty but not mad.

I had a very difficult time when my mother was diagnosed and when she was going through her chemo. I wanted for a long time, probably for the two years that she was going through it, for my cancer to come back. So when I went to the doctor for my checkup, part of me, in a weird way, wanted them to tell me that my cancer had come back, because I felt I had gotten off too easy. I wanted to go through the chemo with her as she was going through it, as her body was just getting destroyed by it. I had gotten off way too easy. It may have been different if I hadn't watched my mother go through what she did just one year after I had been diagnosed. Things may have been a little different with regard to that guilt. But it was definitely something that took me a long time to deal with. To be honest, I think it was that scare in November of this past year that really made me finally let go of some of it. I thought, "Finally I'm going to have to deal with what I'm going to have to deal with," meaning I was finally going to have to get through chemo. Now, with a definite possibility, it was put up or shut up. And I think it took that scare to make me realize, "All right, suck it up. Don't feel sorry for yourself. Move on."

I'm very thankful that I moved up to be with my mom when she got sick. I was there to help my dad and just to be with her. It was great to be able to go over any night of the week and have dinner over there, or take her to the hospital if my dad needed help or something like that. Having had cancer and having had the experiences of being in a hospital and having a checkup and getting my blood taken made it easy for me to be there with her when she went through it. It afforded me a weird bond with her, in that we were able to kind of deal with it together and help each other, you know, talk about this thing called cancer. I think until you actually have cancer, you can't really understand. It changes you in subtle ways.

Losing a parent, whether you've had cancer or not, affects you deeply. Obviously, everybody's different, but I think it affected me pretty heavily. I think it affected me more than if I hadn't had cancer. That guilt was so intense. I felt that I got off easy and that she was the one who had really gone through the tough stuff. You know, there's a difference between being twenty-five, having testicular cancer, and thinking you can take on the world, and being older with a late-stage lung cancer. I never had a doubt that I was going to beat it. But compare that to a woman who's told she's got six months to live. It's a different battle for sure. Definitely a different battle.

Along with the guilt, I've dealt with depression, which I'm sure is a result of a combination of things. I've battled depression probably for the past four years. I think a large part of the reason is my mother's illness and death. Another part is that there's some hereditary predisposition for depression. But I've seen a counselor. I've seen a psychiatrist. I'm on medication. I see a psychologist. When my mother was going through her cancer, there was a really great guy at the hospital who was head of the psychiatry unit for like twenty years. He had retired but still saw terminally ill patients. So my mother started to see him. And we would go in as a family and talk about the issues. My mom's biggest thing was that she wanted to be at peace with each of her kids and her husband before she died. So we would go in once every two weeks as a family. I went a couple of times with my mom by ourselves. My father is more of an "I don't need to see anybody" kind of guy. He just kind of blocks it out. But my mother and I were very much into talking and getting the feelings and issues out in the open. My mom got mad. She got really mad. She said that she felt like cancer was a big bully on the playground coming to kick her ass. And she felt that she didn't really have a fair fight, because it was already Stage IV when she was diagnosed. The lung cancer was in her brain, was in her bones, was in her lung. So she really felt from early on that she was battling an uphill battle. She would say, "This fucking sucks." She'd say, "Shit. This really fucking sucks." And I'd say, "Mom, I hear you." So I think seeing people and talking to people, doing those sorts of things has helped for sure, but I definitely still have to battle depression.

Some of my anger also comes from the fact that my mother was diagnosed with such a late-stage cancer. She had started getting headaches and her speech was slurring. So she felt that something was wrong. She went to the doctor and they thought it might be her thyroid, so they did an X-ray of her neck and the top of her lung was there and they saw this big tumor. She had a bunch of CAT scans, and about five days later they did an MRI of her brain. That's when they told her, "We need to keep you here now, because you've got four tumors in your brain and one of them is butting up against your brain stem. If we hadn't caught this, you probably would have died within a week." And so she had emergency brain surgery. From the get-go she really had a tough time. There were two things that I always felt angry about with regard to my mom dying. One was that she would never get to see me get married and the other was that she would never see my kids, her grandkids. Call them regrets, call them anger, call them whatever. Those were the two major things for me. But my mother and I did have a lot of conversations about these things. She would say, "I've seen four of my kids grow up, be happy and be successful. I've seen two of them get married. I've seen four grandchildren born." She would often say, "I count my blessings." Her last two or three days were terrible. She was in a coma and we had to feed her morphine by mouth. One of us kids would hold her head and the other would inject some morphine into her mouth. Seeing her in that state created a lot of anger. I saw this woman who was mentally and physically in shape become completely debilitated and wrecked. She was sixty-eight years old when she died.

Survivorship means dealing with issues beyond cancer. For me, that would be the retrograde ejaculation. For me, that would be dealing with the guilt of "getting off easy." For me, it means keeping awareness up and keeping that sensitivity of having had cancer and having seen my mother die of a terminal cancer. To me, survivorship in that sense gives me a much deeper appreciation for things, and I think it makes me a much better person.

My name is Tim Madden, I'm twenty-nine years old, and I'm a five-year testicular-cancer survivor.

Live strong.

"Asian women don't get breast cancer."

SUSAN**SHINAGAWA**

I took a class on breast self-exams in 1991. I took it because a friend of mine was teaching it and she asked me to show up. That was the only reason I went, though I should have been going for my own health. I was over the age of thirty and hadn't had any kids. After the class, I was actually very diligent about doing a breast self-exam every month. Six months later, I found a lump that just kind of popped up out of nowhere. And following the instruction of my class, I followed it for two months to see if it made any changes during my menstrual cycle, and it didn't. At the time, I was about to go on a personal leave of absence from work, so I thought that at the same time I was having my teeth cleaned and getting my eyes checked, I ought to have this lump checked out. So I went to see a doctor, and she looked at it and said, "Well, you know, I'm not really worried about it, but since we can feel it, let's go get a mammogram." It was negative. But because it was palpable, meaning we could feel it, the diagnostic radiologist said, "Well, let's do a sonogram." So we did a sonogram and she found that it was a solid mass. So she in turn sent me to see a cancer surgeon. He examined my breast and looked at the negative mammogram. We talked about my family history. And he said to me, "Susan, I don't think you have anything to worry about. You're too young to have breast cancer. You have no family history of cancer. And besides, Asian women don't get breast cancer." So I'm thinking this is what you want to hear when you're young. You don't want to have breast cancer. But I got home that night and I kept thinking. I really do believe in women's intuition, and this little voice in my head was telling me there was something wrong here. The doctor had said that if I lowered my intake of caffeine, the lumps would go away. And I wrote him a note that night that said, "I don't drink coffee. I don't drink tea. I don't drink sodas. I don't like chocolate. I don't take aspirin because I don't like to swallow pills. And I really don't think I can lower my intake of caffeine anymore. Won't you please do a biopsy? I'm about to go on a personal leave of absence. And while I have insurance, it'd be nice to get it done." He found me in the hall the next day at the medical center and said, "Susan, you have to trust me. I see thousands of young women like you every year, and you do not have breast cancer. And I absolutely refuse to do a biopsy." So I'm thinking to myself again, "Okay. He's the expert."

I went on my personal leave of absence. But then there was another thing about my lump. It hurt. In 1991, the belief in the medical community was that if you had a breast lump and it hurt, there was no way it could be cancer, because breast cancer doesn't hurt. So a lot of people were telling me, "You're just being paranoid. Don't worry about it. You're just thinking about it, because you're doing these breast self-exams." But the pain kept it in the forefront of my mind. So, two months later, I decided I was going to get a second opinion. And I went to another university medical center, where they conducted clinical cancer trials, and saw another surgeon. He looked at my films and he did an exam and said that he agreed with the first surgeon that he didn't think I had anything to worry about. In fact, he said, "I could tell you with 99.9 percent accuracy that you do not have breast cancer." Well, of course, I had already decided that I was not going to take no for an answer, so I told him that I wanted to be 100 percent sure. I wanted the biopsy. So he did an incisional biopsy a couple of days later. I was awake for the surgery. I was just under a local anesthetic. So he asked me if I wanted to see the lump, and I said, "Yes." So he brought it over and showed it to me, said, "Absolutely, you don't have anything to worry about. This is definitely not a cancer." And I asked him how he knew, and he said that there was so much fat growing around the lump that it had to have been there at least ten years, and he was very sure it wasn't a breast cancer. "Go home. Live a happy life." So I went home, had breakfast. I was delighted.

Next day, I get a phone call. I had actually been out looking for a job and I came home about five-thirty. There was a message on the answering machine from the surgeon telling me, "Susan, please call me at this number. And if you can't reach me there, call me at this number. And if you can't reach me there, page me at this number." I was pretty sure that he didn't have good news for me, since he insisted that I find him. And, of course, when I called him, he said, "Susan, I'm very sorry to tell you, but you have breast cancer." He was very shocked. He told me that when he got the call from the pathology lab that he was quite certain that they had switched my specimen with somebody else's. He actually walked to the lab to check for himself.

I totally freaked out. My first reaction was, "Oh, my god, I've got breast cancer. I'm going to die a horrible death!" And then I thought, "Oh, my god, I've got breast cancer. It's going to be really bad. I'm going to commit suicide." And then I thought, "Oh, my god, I've got breast cancer. I'd better do something about it." I'm sure these thoughts went through my head in a matter of seconds, but I very clearly remember having them. I worked at a medical center. I didn't know a lot about cancer, but I was intelligent and educated. But still I had this knee-jerk reaction. It really surprised me that I reacted that way. But I very soon decided that I was going to do something about it.

I ended up speaking to a woman who I had met right before I left my job at the medical center to go on my leave. She had just started working there as a patient ombudsman for the cancer center. The only thing I knew about her was that she was about my age and had had cancer. So I got her phone number, called her up, and left a message for her. She called me back a day later, and we talked on the phone for about an hour and a half. And after that conversation, I hung up the phone and my feeling was, I can do this. I can do this. The best thing I did was talk to somebody else who had been there. It really instilled confidence in me that this was going to be a challenge, but not a problem.

I went to the library and checked out about fourteen books, which I read in two days. I wanted to know as much about what I was dealing with as I possibly could. I read a lot about statistics. It's kind of a trap that you fall into as a patient, because you think you want to know the statistics. But you learn later on that statistics really don't mean anything, because when it comes to you, it's always 100 percent. Still, the statistics are very alluring. What is the chance of the breast cancer coming back? What's my chance that I'm going to die? What's my chance that I'm going to live? I figured that at the age of thirty-four and having a premenopausal breast cancer, the risk of the breast cancer coming back sometime throughout my life was probably about 30 percent. But I didn't want to have to worry about this. And I had small breasts. I never identified myself by my breasts. I think in American society, we're kind of socialized to think that breasts are the be-all-end-all physical attribute. Well, that wasn't the way it was for me. So I didn't care about whether or not I kept it. What I did care about was not having to worry about this 30 percent chance of this cancer coming back. So I decided to have a mastectomy. It was an informed decision that I made on my own. I really thought hard about it.

After that I wanted to follow up my surgery with adjuvant chemotherapy. I was told by a number of oncologists that I was just being hysterical and paranoid. But I was not going to take no for an answer. I had already learned not to take no for an answer once. And so I had eight cycles of chemotherapy. I continued to do a lot of reading of the medical literature while I was in treatment. In the middle of my treatment, the first reports were just coming out saying that there was a definite significant survival advantage for premenopausal women with early-stage breast cancer who had surgery followed by adjuvant chemotherapy. I felt totally vindicated. I was surprised that all these people were telling me that I was being crazy for wanting it.

I did really well with my treatment. I never thought I was going to have any problem with cancer again. One day I was home cooking dinner, and while the food was on the stove, I sat down at the couch to watch the nightly news. And I remember very specifically that I started to get this pain in my left hip. And it got worse and worse and worse through the night. I couldn't get rid of it. It was one of those pains where at first I thought it was just the position I was sitting in, but I couldn't get it to go away. And it was so bad that I couldn't sleep. The next morning I felt fine. But one week later, the exact same thing happened. Cooking dinner, sitting on the couch, looking at the television to watch the evening news, and the pain starts again, except this time, not only is it in my hip, but it's all the way down my left leg. The next day I went to work but the pain was still really bothering me. I called up my primary physician. She had me come in right away. I never went back to work after that day. She started me on a whole bunch of diagnostic tests. I was taking four and five different tests and procedures every day. Within two weeks, the entire left side of my body was either numb or weak. My foot was drooping. The left side of my face was drooping. My left retina was unresponsive. I was in a wheelchair and in a whole lot of pain. And it turns out that I was diagnosed with recurrent breast cancer, but it had appeared in my cerebral spinal fluid. Not a good thing to have.

It's funny, because this whole time my doctors were thinking about a recurrence of cancer, it never even occurred to me. Never occurred to me once. I don't know why. I guess I had always assumed that if I had a recurrence, it was going to be in the breast and it was going to be something that was really obvious to me.

This time it was a whole slew of different treatments. Before the recurrence was actually diagnosed, they had started me on a high dose of steroids. I remember the doctor telling me that I might gain a few pounds. So eighty-seven pounds later, I had surgery to have an Ommaya catheter implanted in my brain, through which I received chemotherapy every day. I also had radiation to my lumbar spine, because they had done some other test that showed there was some blockage of my cerebral spinal fluid. Every day for five weeks, I was getting radiation and chemotherapy that they would inject through the catheter in my brain. The chemo made me sicker than a dog. I'd never been so nauseated in my life. And with the radiation on top of that, because it was hitting my intestines and my stomach, made it just really horrible. At that point, I didn't want to finish treatment. It was just unbearable. But I finally got through it. After I had all the radiation and treatment, the weakness of my left side resolved itself.

My advocacy work is a direct result of my experience of being diagnosed with my cancer and what I went through trying to get treatment for my cancer and my cancer pain. In the beginning, I started out speaking up about young women being diagnosed with cancer. Everyone is telling you that young women don't get breast cancer. Certainly, cancer is a disease primarily of older people. And the percentages, again, for young women who get breast cancer are small, but I think it's an absolute lie and disservice to tell young women that they don't have to worry about it. So that was the first thing I started speaking out about. And then it occurred to me, gee, how many Asian women are being told that they don't have to worry about a lump, because Asian women don't get breast cancer? So I read up on that. And what I found out is that the statistics that say young Asian women don't get breast cancer are all based on the National Cancer Institute data, which is collected nationwide. The problem with that data is that it doesn't take into account the demographics of the Asian-American population, which is about 70 percent first-generation immigrant. Asian immigrants *coming from* the Asian countries in the world have the lowest breast-cancer rates globally. So when you take that into account, what you're reporting on in the United States in terms of breast-cancer rates for Asian women are the breast-cancer rates of first-generation women who come from the countries with the lowest breast-cancer rates. Those statistics don't report on someone like me who was born here. My parents were born here, I'm third-generation Japanese-American. Last year, there was a report that came out in Los Angeles that showed the rates of breast cancer in Japanese-American women, out of all ethnicities in Los Angeles County, are rising faster than any other ethnic group. I think that's pretty alarming. But in talking to other Asian women, they're all still getting that same story: that they don't have to worry because Asian women don't get breast cancer. So I have a lot more work to do. But over the past twelve years, it's been one of my major messages. It doesn't matter who you are or what you look like, what your ethnicity is, you are at risk for breast cancer.

There are a number of challenges in trying to advocate in terms of cancer in general in Asian communities. One of those challenges is just this prevailing belief that Asians don't have to worry about cancer. Nothing could be further from the truth. Aside from the fact that everybody is at risk for getting breast cancer, there are some cancers that occur predominantly in Asians. Two of those are stomach and liver cancer. One of the main reasons people get liver cancer is because of the Hepatitis B infection, and Asian immigrants have the highest rates of Hepatitis B in the world. And all you need to do is get a vaccination for it, but not enough people are getting that vaccination. Unfortunately, Hepatitis B is passed down from a mother to her child, so the earlier Hepatitis B is contracted, the greater the chance of getting liver cancer later on in life. And it's sad, because it's highly preventable.

It's really important that you be an advocate for yourself or find somebody who's willing to advocate for you. Unfortunately, you don't really learn this until you go through the whole experience of having cancer and having to deal with the medical community. Certainly, there are some wonderful doctors out there, but in general the medical establishment, in my opinion, is going to try to get by with as little as they possibly can. You have to demand the right treatment, you have to demand quality treatment, and you have to demand that they listen to you. Sometimes they don't like it when you do that, but you have to do it.

My name is Susan. I was diagnosed with breast cancer in 1991. I had a recurrence in 1997. And I was diagnosed with a second primary breast cancer in 2001.

And I'm still here.

Live strong.

"Be strong in accepting help."

MORTIMER**BROWN**

My name is Mortimer Brown. I was diagnosed with colorectal cancer in September of 1999.

My surgery came immediately because it was an emergency. One night I saw the toilet bowl full of blood. I went to the hospital that night and had surgery the next day. I didn't have a lot of time to ponder and wonder. I really don't remember quite a bit from those days. I remember going to the hospital. I remember being admitted. And I remember the next day having my physician come down with a lot of other people to look at me to see what was causing the bleeding. They found a mass. My wife says that they talked about surgery and that at first I was reluctant. But she said that they then advised me that if I didn't, I would likely die from loss of blood. But I don't remember any of that.

My advice to someone about to undergo the surgery I went through would be to feel mentally secure and confident. Know that your surgeons and your other caretakers, your physicians and so on, are the best. If you don't have that confidence, don't have the surgery. Find someone in whom you can have that confidence. Find a man or a woman surgeon who you can talk to, who can tell you something about what's going to happen so that you can go in with ease and with comfort.

You won't remember the surgery, of course. You'll be under

anesthetic. And when you come out, it will be a surprise. All of a sudden you'll awaken. You'll look around and discover that there are tubes in your arm, maybe something in your nose, and things are . . . well, it'll feel very, very different. It'll feel bizarre. Someone will be there, your wife, your children perhaps, and they'll want to talk to you. They'll be very concerned about you. You'll be concerned about yourself. But if you can, try to put them at ease, and then they will feel comfortable, which will make you feel more comfortable.

There will be physical trouble. There will be some pain. There will be some dryness of the mouth. You won't be able to eat the way you ordinarily would. But little by little, your appetite and diet will return. The nurses will be coming and going. They'll be doing something and then in the middle of it, they'll say, "I'll be right back." Off they go, and you don't see them again for a week. "I'll be right back" has become kind of a joke in my family. If I'm going out to get the newspaper or something, I'll say to my wife, "I'll be right back." She says, "Okay. See you in July."

But the physical concomitants of surgery are a real nuisance. They are hard. But you do get over them. I think having the right attitude and knowing that I'm going to get over the physical issues has helped me to get past them. If I focus on the pain and the strain and the distress, it only intensifies those feelings and delays getting past them.

As part of my surgery, they took out a considerably large piece of my colon and they sewed up my rectum. To be indelicate for a minute, you can no longer call me that nasty name, because I haven't got one. When my body needs to excrete feces, since I don't have a rectum, I have a hole in my side that's connected to my intestine. Connected to that is a wafer and a bag, and I excrete right into the bag. In the early days of coming back from surgery, that proved to be a real problem. I felt dirty. I felt smelly. I felt that everybody knew about what I was dealing with. And worst of all, I felt that my body was totally distorted.

I felt very unkind about my body image. Following that, a year or so later, because of the changes inside my body and the pieces they took out and the rearranging of my organs, I had a hernia that had to be corrected. Since then, my body has been very much disrupted internally. Things are not in their ordinary places, and from time to time that's a nuisance. But when I consider the alternative, those issues are trivial. I've mellowed. When I ask myself "Well, would you rather hang around and do what you're doing like this, or would you rather just be gone?," the answer is easy. I do not want to be gone. I want to hang around.

I experienced two big physical changes when I got out of the hospital. One was that I was very tired. There's a condition, something called cancer-related fatigue, that I've come to know well. I was tired and had very little energy. Of course that worried me, made me anxious, made me upset. But it's something to be expected after surgery when you get home, though it is something that you grow out of somewhat. Your body adapts and recalibrates to normal. The fatigue comes back, goes away, comes and goes, but eventually you get beyond that. The other large physical issue was the ostomy bag. Getting used to that was very difficult. It was a mental problem at first, the idea of having that bag in my side. But then it was a physical problem. The actual manipulation of the bag felt like a daily ordeal. I had to deal with practical issues like where to get them. You just don't go into Wal-Mart and look on the shelf and find ostomy bags. Although, if they were there one of these days, ha, it wouldn't surprise me, the way they're expanding. But I had to get in touch with a hospital-supply organization and get on their mailing list and so on. And there are different kinds of bags and supplies. According to the size of the stoma—that's the opening into the intestine—you have to cut the wafer in order to make it fit properly. That proved to be somewhat of a problem for me in those early days. I'll tell you right now, I hope that you have a wife or a significant other who can help as a caregiver. It's most essential that you have someone around who can help you with that. Just manipulating the bag and then learning how to put it on, learning how to clean around the stoma, all of those are issues that you'll need to know about. And you'll get anxious about it, and you'll be upset. "Oh, my God, how am I going to do this?!" At first, it's like any new thing, like learning a keyboard or anything else. It's frustrating. It's annoying. And you'll say, "Why did this happen to me?" Let those things pass. You'll learn how to do it. I've now had it for a little over four years, and it's become routine. It's no longer a big, serious physical problem. Every now and then I look at my body and still get upset and annoyed, but considering the alternative, I'd rather have this burden than not.

I am grateful to have Marilyn, my wife, with me, to help and be my caregiver. We've been married for fifty-nine years, though that's only a small part of it. We've known each other since we were kids in fourth grade. We got married while I was in the army during World War II. We were young. I was twenty-one. She was twenty. And so we've grown, matured, and developed together. We've grown and developed our tastes in art and literature together. We've developed our attitudes toward politics and the world together. And we've grown in such a way that we've given and taken from each other over the years in many ways. When she became ill a few years ago, I helped her and cared for her and looked after her. When our children were born, I participated and helped in their care. We had those experiences together.

So when cancer appeared in our family, in our life, in my body, it was another sort of opportunity. It was another event in what was by then a long series of interactions of support. Nevertheless, it called for much more of a commitment than any of our previous emergencies or trials. I don't remember this, but my wife tells me that she and my son Mark were in the hospital room when I was coming out of the anesthetic, I looked at them and saw the terrible stress and distress on their faces. And as I looked at them I said, "Don't worry. I'm going to lick this thing." I don't remember that at all, but my son confirms that that's what took place. So when we got home from the hospital, I already had in my guts the affirmation that I was going to lick this thing.

In the hospital, they were very perfunctory in giving us instructions about things to do and how to do them. Over the years since then, we feel a little sad about that and have tried once or twice to go back to the hospital and tell the ostomy nurse and some of the other people about things that would have been useful to know. But it proves futile. I think that every hospital ought to have an ombudsman or a patient-care advisor, someone to whom a patient can turn and say, "I need this," or, "I don't understand that." Because the nurses and staff are very, very busy. Hospitals used to be places for caring for patients. Now they're places to make money for the management and for the stockholders. The nurses are overburdened, the aides are not as well trained as they should be, and a lot of things slide by. At least, that's been my experience. When we got home, we hardly knew anything about how to take care of me and how to perform some of the basic procedures that were to become part of my daily life.

So my wife did a lot of research. We got some literature. We're both academically inclined, so the first thing we did was go to the literature. I also tried to find out if there was a support group that could provide information. I learned that there were support groups for women who had had breast cancer, for men who had had prostate cancer, for people with skin cancer, people who'd had laryngectomies . . . but there were no support groups for people with colorectal cancer. Eventually, I started one, but at the outset, there was no place that we could turn to for support and information. It was pretty much on-the-job training. My wife took the lead in the learning and in the doing and taught me.

To this very day, she is my stalwart. She helps me in all things that need to happen. Thank God I don't need as much now as

I did the first month after I came out of the hospital. And I've been able to reciprocate. We're both older guys, and now and then she gets down with arthritis or other things that bother her. Fortunately, I can help her. I'm still the man about the house. I can reach the high shelves. I open the hard bottles. I can still do those kinds of things. But in the main, she stands beside me in helping with anything that's related to my cancer.

I feel extremely fortunate to have my wife. I learned something yesterday that broke my heart, to tell the truth. I heard a lady talking about being alone when she was recovering. My mind raced. How would I have done it if I were alone? I think I would have sunk into despair or become severely depressed. I thank my wife, my caregiver, for the blessing that I did not have to face it alone. When we've talked about that, she's said, "You could have done it. You're a strong guy. You've done other difficult things before." And I've said, "Maybe you're right. I might have been able to, but it would have been a much different journey and I would have ended up somewhere else."

After I came home from the hospital, I was aware that I was a different guy. By the time of my surgery, I'd already retired from my own practice, but I was doing some part-time teaching at different colleges and universities in the area. I was an adjunct professor of psychology. I got to wondering whether I could continue doing that kind of work. I shortly came to realize that I could and that I was going to. I wanted to do that. I knew from experience and from my interests that it would help me to not seclude myself from being involved in things. And it was during those early times in those discussions with myself that I came to realize that what I needed to do was grab on to life and remain active. And that was essentially what I did.

The last treatment I had was surgery. My life has been very different since my surgery. I have a different point of view about what I do, with whom I do it, and for how long I have to do it. My wife says I've mellowed. What she means by that is that

I don't take things as seriously as I used to. I've stopped trying to fix the world. I let things go. I notice differences in my own self. I notice that I'm more attentive to things that would normally just pass me by. I'm more in touch with nature. I'm more in touch with spiritual matters. And I'm more in touch with the people around me, even in trivial or day-to-day things. I enjoy being in touch and being a caring and sharing person. I've been like that before, but it's much more intense now, and I notice it much more. It makes me feel good.

Before my diagnosis, I knew very little about cancer. I had seen the ads from the American Cancer Society and other groups and I'd made contributions from time to time. But I was mostly ignorant. One of the things that I discovered in my research was that people who were involved in support groups had a richer and fuller return to life. Some of the studies tentatively suggested that they prolonged life, especially in support groups for women who had breast cancer. The data were controversial but were clear, however, that women who went to support groups lived richer and fuller lives than those who did not. There was no support group in my area for colorectal cancer. So I did some research to learn how to start a support group and started one. I became active in the American Cancer Society. I wanted to do more and went down there and asked, "What can I do to help?" They gave me a list of volunteer activities. I signed up to be a driver for patients who needed to go to a hospital or to treatment who couldn't drive themselves or didn't have anybody to drive them. And so I drove some patients from time to time. Every one of them was amazed when they learned that I was also a survivor, because all the other drivers they had had in the past were volunteers but not cancer survivors. And that kind of made me a little bit proud. I felt good about that and wanted to do more of that kind of thing. I also became an American Cancer Society advocate. I participated in helping organize and be part of the Relay for Life, a fund-raising activity where we organize people and then walk around a track at a local high school. I also helped them organize and develop the support group that we came to call "The Semicolons," because we share the experience of having had a chunk of our colon cut out.

"Keeping busy" is too superficial an expression. That implies busywork. Keeping involved is more than just being busy. It is being involved intellectually. I'm an old guy and I don't want to deteriorate mentally. So I keep myself involved intellectually and emotionally. I make appointments with my grandson to keep that contact. He's now eighteen. When he was younger, he'd come over every weekend. We'd play. We'd roll on the floor when he was little. We'd go to the circus. I'd take him to see movies that he wanted to see. We'd do all that. Now he's eighteen. He's in a little rock band. He's got a girlfriend. He's busy at school. Nevertheless, we have our appointments and we keep our contact.

At first with friends and strangers, I felt a little bit like I was walking on eggshells, as it were. People were very tentative around me. But that's gone away. I don't think that's the case anymore, and I'm glad of it. New survivors talk in our support group sometimes about people pitying them. I never felt pitied in that sense. I did have a sense that people were interested and curious. And when I let them know that I was willing to discuss the experience, they came to me and asked questions. But I've never in any sense been discriminated against or put down. But neither, at the other end of the spectrum, have I been ennobled or made to feel special. I think I take my survivorship as a matter of fact. People seem to accept that from me and treat me accordingly. I think the way people treat someone who has had cancer has a lot to do with the survivor and his or her own attitude about themselves. If you go around pitying yourself, you're going to get either rejection or pity from others. Group meetings are entirely different of course. There, a discussion is put to the floor. That's what the group is for. But in my poker group, it's no big deal. I hardly mention it. I don't think that people "treat me differently" because I'm a survivor.

I do treat myself differently, though, in a lot of ways. When I was a boy growing up during the Depression, my father was out of work and my family was short of wherewithal and funds. So I adopted an early attitude of saving and not spending. Saving for a rainy day. I didn't learn until much, much later, though, that I could also spend on a sunny day. It's still difficult for me to do that. So as a survivor, every now and then I'll tell myself, "You can afford another tie, or an extra candy bar, or a better grade of beer, or whatever. Let yourself do that." It's still difficult to do that. My wife says that I'm generous with other people. She thinks I tip too much in restaurants. But I remember when I was in college and I had part-time jobs. I can afford another buck, and those people find it useful and necessary. So I find myself more easygoing in that way, and I attribute part of that to being a survivor. I'm grateful to be around and want to help where I can.

People will want to help you as well. I had mixed feelings about it. I didn't feel that I needed help, and I also worried that they were only helping me because they pitied me. I also felt that if I accepted help it meant that I wasn't strong. I wasn't manly. I wasn't virile. But I got past these things by asking myself, "If someone else needed your help, would you offer it?" Of course I would. "Would I feel good if they accepted it?" You bet. So give people a chance to feel good. Accept it, especially from your wife or caregiver. They want to help. Don't demean it. Don't say, "I don't need it." Be strong in accepting help.

I don't feel guilty that I survived cancer, nor do I rail against God for doing this to me. I'm grateful that I'm past it and grateful for the help that I've had getting past it. People have asked me, when I first was diagnosed with cancer, was I anxious and worried and fearful of death? I didn't have the time to be anxious, worried, or fearful. I learned that I had cancer one Monday morning, and by Monday evening or the next Tuesday morning, I was in surgery. The effect of the information began to drift in once I was out of surgery. Of course, I was anxious. We grew up thinking cancer is a killer. And I thought, "Oh my God, I don't want to die. I've got too much yet to do." I saw the anxiety in the face of my wife and my son in the hospital, and I became anxious and fearful. But I'm not anxious and fearful now. In the four or so years since then, I've become aware that death is always a possibility. When we're young, intellectually we know that we're all going to die someday, but we live nevertheless as though we won't.

I'm almost eighty years old. I made a deal with God that I'm going to live to be ninety. Why ninety? When my grandson was little, five or six years old, we were having a wonderful time playing ninja soldiers rolling on the floor and tickling and teasing. And one time after he caught his breath he said, "Oh, Grandpa, wait. Wait a minute. Wait a minute. Grandpa, when I'm a man and I have a boy, you and I and my little boy will all play like this together. Promise me, Grandpa. Promise me." So I made him a promise. I said, "Okay, I'll try, but I'm kind of old, Nick. And when you're a man and have a boy, I'll be very, very old, and I'm not sure that I'll still be around. You understand, right?" "Well, Grandpa, you just try and I'll try to help." Who could not grab that kid and hug him and be full of joy? So I said, "Okay, I'll try and you'll help." So now at this stage of my life and being a cancer survivor, I need to try hard and make certain that I am doing everything possible to keep that promise.

Every now and then I do get anxious, especially at meetings, when so many people talk about recurrence. I'm grateful, thankful, full of richness and warmness that I've not had a recurrence, but there's always a chance of having one. If I do, I'll get past it. So my anxiety is not so much about dying as it is more focused on the possibility of recurrence and the possibility of being taken out of my daily activities, my life, and having to go back into the hospital.

I noticed yesterday in some of the literature of the Lance Armstrong Foundation that *carpe diem* is part of the rubric. Shortly after I came out of the hospital and vowed that I was going to go on and continue living, I adopted the notion of *carpe vitam*. That means "seize life." That's my motto. I try to pass that along to people every day. Seizing today, of course, is the traditional motto. Yes, take the day and do it. But seizing life, life and all of its meaning and its richness, came to be for me what I'm all about and how I want to live.

I'm a member of a special club. It just occurred to me. We are all of us grateful to be in the club. We paid our dues and continue paying our dues. For me, as an individual in that club, survivorship is twofold. I'm happy, grateful, aware of myself that I have the strength and the will to be a survivor and to continue as a survivor. At the same time, however, I'm humble in the face of the fact that I've had a lot of help in my survivorship: the surgeons, oncologists, my wife as caregiver, my sons and grandson, friends, all of those who have had a part in my daily life as a survivor. I don't wake up every morning and say, "Oh, I'm a cancer survivor again today." I live my life. Every now and then I'm reminded that I'm a cancer survivor. And during the times when I go to my support groups and volunteer, I focus on survivorship. But mainly I see myself as who I am. And survivorship is just one more aspect of my sense of self. I'm grateful to be a survivor, grateful for the people who've helped me to continue to be a survivor, and want to continue to participate in survivorship activities. I identify as a survivor.

My name is Mortimer Brown, I'm seventy-nine years old, and I'm a four-year survivor of colorectal cancer.

Live strong.

"The survival rates are 100 percent for Scott Toner."

SCOTT**TONER**

On December 11, 2000, I was diagnosed with a neuroendocrine tumor of the pancreas.

I had given blood at the Red Cross in September of 2000. Two or three weeks afterward, they came back to me and said that they thought I might have hepatitis because my enzyme levels were so high. So for the next three months, my doctor was going over my body trying to determine what was going on. I went through a lot of different biopsies and tests to try to figure out exactly what I had. I don't think the doctor could conceive of the fact that I had cancer, especially because what I had was so rare. At first, he thought that I had liver cancer because the tumor there was so large. He diagnosed me, and I went to see a lot of different liver-cancer specialists. I saw one of the best liver-transplant specialists in the world. He basically said that if I had liver cancer, it was pretty much over because it was so spread out within my liver. But what they eventually figured out was that I really had a neuroendocrine tumor of the pancreas, which is a slightly slower-growing form of cancer that responds to different types of treatment than does liver cancer. What had really happened was that the cancer had grown from my pancreas. It was such a small tumor that, compared to the metastasis in the liver, it made it look like what I had was liver cancer. There was a well-known specialist in Boston who knew

a lot about this form of cancer. I went through the normal protocol. They were hoping that they could shrink the tumor
enough to surgically resect it. But that didn't work. We stopped
the treatments and decided to treat it palliatively. They were
just sort of hoping to give me a little bit of extra time. But then
I got into a clinical trial for Endostatin, which I've been on for
a little over two years now. My tumor has been stable since
then. I have a little bit more hope that this might be the miracle drug that could truly treat cancer more as a chronic disease,
like diabetes, where you just give yourself a shot every day.

In this clinical trial, what I've been doing is basically giving
myself a shot of Endostatin twice a day and seeing my doctor
every two weeks. They kind of poke around a little bit, make
sure that the tumor's not growing. I get a CAT scan every two
months. And that's about it. It's good to be so closely monitored. I think the reason they have me visit the doctor so frequently is that they're expecting something bad to happen, like
all of a sudden I'm going to say, "I feel miserable. I'm really fatigued. I have all these horrible symptoms." But that's not
what's happening. Instead, I'm going in and saying, "I feel perfectly fine." Protocol says that they have to make sure that I'm
fine, so they check me out and make sure that the tumor isn't
growing. That's about it. One of the side effects I'm having
from going every few weeks is that I'm starting to get sort of
upset when I have to go in. I think that's just great. I've gotten
past the "Thank God, I'll do anything to get treated for this
cancer" phase, to now all of a sudden becoming upset that
I have to go in and see a doctor every two weeks. I think
that's good.

Right from the get-go I took off nine months from work and
went on disability. When I came back, they made sure I had a
job. They even send a courier to pick up my drugs every two
weeks, and they never question me when I have to leave to go
to the doctor. They really have been terrific. Thinking more
long-term, though, I worry about insurance. I'm confident

working for my current company, but if I ever lost my job or wanted to move to another company, there are serious questions about the future that I need to consider. Will the other company give me insurance? I'm not sure. That's limiting because I've kept myself from even thinking about getting another job at another company for that reason alone. Luckily, the company I'm with is very large, with a lot of different jobs and opportunities that I could switch around to.

The doctors never said, "You're going to die," or anything like that. They were trying their hardest to cure me. But without them even saying it, I knew that there was only so much they could do. I learned from reading the literature that if they could get my tumor to shrink a little bit, then they could go in and resect it and get it out of my liver. But with the size of that tumor, there wasn't going to be a cure for what I had. I think one of the best pieces of advice my first oncologist ever gave me was, "Don't look at the statistics, because you never know what's going to happen. Every person is a unique individual." And I stuck by that. I try not to look at the odds or statistics of what the average life expectancy is for someone who is diagnosed with this particular form of cancer. As my doctor was explaining, there are so many variables for each person that you can't truly predict how one person's disease will progress. Age is a large determining factor. For example, I'm much younger than a lot of people who are diagnosed with cancer. So trying to compare me to a seventy-year-old man who has been diagnosed with what I have, it's not going to mean much. The statistics won't work. And so what I've learned to do is just say, "Okay. I'm my own person, and as long as I survive, then the survival rates are 100 percent for Scott Toner."

One thing that cancer has helped me to realize is that I just have to enjoy life even though I could die at any time. Everyone's going to die at some point, so you might as well enjoy what you have now. And that's what I've done. I began to enjoy what was right there in front of me. I've accepted that I can either enjoy the life that I have or I can sit here and worry about how much longer I have. I did go to a lot of different support groups. I realized that one of the strange things that happens to some cancer survivors is after they're cured and they get a clean bill, they become even more obsessed with death. They become even more upset about the fact that they had cancer than when they were actually going through it. I know part of it has to do with fighting so hard through cancer and then being left with nothing except, "Now what?" There's also the fear of recurrence and having to go through it all once again. But my attitude has been that everyone is going to die someday. It just seems that survivors have been given a sort of gift of having death put in front of them. They've already confronted it and come to grips with the fact that they're going to die someday just like everyone else. So they enjoy it while they can. Death is abstract before illness and trauma and becomes real after being diagnosed. You know that sooner or later you have to face it. As long as you start enjoying your life, confronting death is not the most terrible thing.

I think I've enjoyed my life more since I was diagnosed. I realize that a lot of the smaller things don't matter. For example, I manage a group of people at work, and ironically, I'm the one who usually tells them to relax and not get so upset about things, and not to work too much overtime. There are bigger things to be concerned about than completing a work project. We'll get it done. We'll take care of it. But to stress out about it the whole time is not the way to go through life. I think that those are the good things to finally put into the right perspective. Once you realize that you don't have complete control over your life, even though you want to and think that you do, you can let go and get on with living. Cancer is good at showing you that. What you can control is how you react to certain things. And so I try to control how I react more than I try to control the situation. I'm never going to tell my body to just get rid of the cancer. It's there. Maybe someday there will be a cure that will completely remove it, but at the moment, there isn't, so I must be responsible for how I'm reacting to having and living with it.

Caregiving was rough for my family because when I was first diagnosed, they all wanted to do something for me. They were going to all my doctor's appointments and trying to do everything with me. One of my brothers would cry in the doctor's lobby for the whole appointment. And so I finally told them that they should stop coming, because they were more of a burden than a support. During the chemotherapy, I didn't really have terrible side effects, so they didn't need to take care of me even then. I think they felt more helpless than I did. At least I had the chemotherapy. I had something to do that I could point to and say, "I'm doing this. I'm making this effort. I'm doing something to fight this disease." They couldn't go out and create a cure for cancer or anything like that on their own. So what we did to help them feel less powerless was start doing fundraisers. That helped them feel like they were at least doing something to fight the disease. I think it really helped them. We've done an annual fund-raiser for the past three years. They get really involved in trying to raise money for cancer. So that was my main caregiver concern.

I was really concerned about dating after I was diagnosed. I didn't have a girlfriend at the time, and I didn't think it was fair to anyone to get involved when I was first diagnosed because I was so focused on fighting the disease. When I got into the Endostatin trial, I started to feel like there might be a cure. And so I started dating. Even then, I was concerned about how she was going to react when I finally told her that I had cancer. What surprised me was that there was no reaction like, "Oh, you have cancer. Well, then I don't want to go out with you," or anything like that. It was fine to her. She was willing to accept it. Now we're engaged and getting married in September. Instead of worrying about how people are going to react or trying to control the situation, I just went out on a limb and said, "I like you. Let's get married." She never had concerns about what was going to happen to me two years down the road. I think about it from my parents' perspectives. My father passed away at a very young age from a heart attack. And I wonder, "Would my mother not have gone out with my father if she knew that ten years into the marriage he was going to die of a heart attack? Would she have given up the relationship, the kids that she had with my father, the life that she lived, just because he was going to die young?" But I know that she would rather have had the ten years with him than to have just completely ended it. There are a lot of good times to be had with people, be it ten, fifty, or just one year before they're gone.

I'm hoping to make history being on the cutting edge with Endostatin. Maybe someday this drug is going to be like insulin. Even though I don't know what's going to happen and am sort of out there, every day I go with my tumor being stable, without it growing, is another day that I'm proving to the FDA that the drug works and that it can help people live. The uncertainty of it all does makes it a little scary, but having already come to terms with death makes it less so. When I was diagnosed, one of the first things they told me was they thought I had liver cancer and that it was fatal. With the Endostatin, I have a chance again. This drug has given me the reassurance that today is probably not going to be the day that I die. But who knows if the FDA is going to approve it? It still has to go through a gauntlet of different trials and receive financial backing to get it out to market. I also happen to have a very, very rare form of cancer, so right now, even though this drug is proving that it works for me and a handful of others, the market might not see the financial incentive for putting it out there. They might end up taking away a drug that truly does work on cancer. I don't think that's going to happen, but it is a possibility. So there are these uncertainties. Again, it makes me realize that if I worry about what's going to happen tomorrow, I can't enjoy today. It's not worth worrying about tomorrow, because a lot of those worries won't even come to fruition. It's better to focus on today, enjoy it, and move on to tomorrow when it happens. One of the gifts of getting cancer is getting that drilled into you—enjoy today.

Don't let a cancer diagnosis dictate that you're bedridden, or that you're not supposed to continue living life. When I was going through the normal chemotherapy, I had some acupuncture. I did some yoga. I was lucky in that I didn't have a lot of side effects from the chemotherapy, though the first week I was incredibly nauseated. The acupuncture did incredible things for me. Once I started it, the nausea went away and I felt a lot better. I think it gets rid of a lot of the symptoms from chemotherapy. I also think it helped that I was in pretty good shape. Exercise helped me to get through chemotherapy, and I still keep up my routine. I've recently slowed down a little on the jogging, but I have run quite a few marathons. I *never* ran any marathons before I was diagnosed with cancer. Basically, every time I've run a marathon I've run it with cancer. I've run six of them. In addition to the marathons, I've done a lot of things since being diagnosed. I've gone to Europe a few times. I've gotten engaged and I'm going to get married. A lot of different things have happened in my life that I could have just as easily sort of rolled up in a ball, said, "I've been diagnosed with cancer. I guess I'm going to die in the next X months," and thrown away. But that's not what has to happen. Every diagnosis is different. You might not have the chance to live to be eighty, but that doesn't mean that you can't still enjoy life for whatever time you have on earth.

What is survivorship? Survivorship is enjoying what you've been given, enjoying the friends and family that you have, and just enjoying the miracle of life. You've been blessed to have it, so just enjoy everything, every minute that you have.

My name is Scott Toner. I'm thirty-five years old, and I'm a four-year survivor of neuroendocrine tumor of the pancreas.

Live strong.

"Put your pride in your back pocket."

ERIC**MILLER**

I became a survivor on June 23, 2000, when my son Garrett was diagnosed with a brain blastoma at age five.

Garrett had to deal with a lot of different physical issues. The brain tumor had to be removed, on June 24, 2000, while he was in the ICU on a ventilator. After surgery he was blind, mute, and paralyzed, so he was in a wheelchair for a while and had to relearn how to walk. He was in speech therapy for months relearning how to speak, and the visual impairment has continued to this day and won't likely resolve itself. So he's learning Braille. He still has a lot of different physical problems that we have to deal with.

The first thing that you have to do as a parent is become as educated as possible. I know that with the diagnosis it's hard to get your thoughts clear, but there are clinical trials that are available. There are treatment options that you can choose from that can really help in the long-term care of your son or daughter. It's important that you have the strength and the wherewithal to really educate yourself on all the different options that are available.

There are so many emotional stages you go through when your child's diagnosed with cancer. It's the classic grief-to-disbelief-to-denial-to-anger-to, finally, acceptance, and you have to allow yourself to go through all those processes. If you don't, you get stuck in one of those and you just never get out of it. They are all natural feelings. Then you realize that things are different. The world has changed now, and it's very difficult to think about life as it used to be. I don't know how we got through it. We just did it, with the help of a lot of other people. That was the hardest thing for me, accepting help from other people, whether it was financial assistance, whether it was cooking us meals, whether it was taking care of our other children. It was difficult allowing other people to help us. And people want to help; they're yearning to help. That was how we were able to deal with a lot of Garrett's physical problems and continue to deal with them. That was really the hardest thing for me as a man, I think. I've got a good job, I've got health insurance, and people started handing me five-hundred-dollar checks and saying, "We're setting up a medical fund," and I tried to stop it.

I finally had a friend who was strong enough to tell me to put my ego in my back pocket and allow people to help me and the family. And the cliché of "it's easier to give than to receive" really became real to me. Taking those checks was hard. Five hundred dollars here, one thousand there from the garage sale that Garrett's T-ball team had for him. What I didn't realize at the beginning was that we were going to need that money. Insurance says that they're going to pay for everything, but then you find out that some of the chemo drugs aren't on their list of approved drugs, and all of a sudden your co-pays go from ten dollars to fifty. There are a lot of other expenses that I didn't know were coming. But fortunately, my friend told me to let go of my ego. When people are trying to do things for you, they're not doing it because they have to. They're doing it because they want to. What I didn't realize was that there were other people who were hurting just as badly as we were, and this was their only way of feeling that they were part of the process of healing and helping. By not allowing them to do that, by keeping that wall around myself, I was really keeping

them out, which made them feel helpless. It was a hard lesson
for me to learn; a very hard lesson.

I can remember when Garrett was diagnosed. It was the lowest
of the lows. I can remember the loneliness and despair, wondering if anybody else in the world felt the way I felt, if anybody cared or understood. I think that a lot of the loneliness of
my cancer experience was a result of not being able to relate.
My wife couldn't relate to what I was going through, and I
couldn't relate to what my wife was going through. I wanted to
be left alone. I didn't want people touching me. I didn't want
to talk to anybody. My wife needed that nurturing, those hugs
and affirmations that everything was going to be okay. It led to
some trials in our marriage, frankly. We weren't taking care of
each other, and it led to a lot of turmoil, to the point that we
started talking about getting a divorce. This disease had not
only infected our son but was now infecting our marriage. Fortunately, we were smart enough to recognize all the stresses and
get some counseling. We got through it. I think that's a real
challenge for married couples; not being able to relate to what
the other person is feeling. It was very difficult. Fortunately,
three years out we're doing fine.

Because Garrett lost his sight, he isn't going to be able to read
like other children. He has enough sight that with a magnifying
TV he can read some print, but not very quickly. They wanted
to start teaching him Braille earlier, but unfortunately, because
of the chemotherapy, he had lost feeling in his fingertips from
something called peripheral neuropathy, so we had to wait. But
just a few weeks ago, he got his Braille writer, and he's starting
to learn to read. He's so excited. It's very exciting for us that
he's going to be able to enjoy reading, because he loves books
on tape now. Reading is so important to developing the mind
and developing a view of the world. So we're excited that he's
finally getting to learn that. He's remarkable in the way he's

recovered and adapted to the blindness. At first it was difficult. It was hard for him to get around. But now you can hardly tell that he's profoundly visually impaired. He just broke his nose last week in New York City. He forgets sometimes that he's visually impaired. He was chasing his brother through the lobby of the hotel and his brother darted into a glass door as it was closing. Garrett could see his brother on the other side, but couldn't see the glass and ran face first into it and broke his nose. You know, when you've had a tumor taken out of your head, a little broken nose isn't too big of a deal. He's so funny. And he's recovering from it.

Garrett's got some remarkable stories. When he lost his hair from the chemo, we had more than two hundred people who I work with, firefighters, police officers, nurses, paramedics, who shaved their heads for him. His brothers and I shaved our heads, too, and our motto became, "When you're as good looking as us, hair is just a crutch." He's got a great sense of humor. He's remarkably perceptive for such a young man. Well, I say "young man." Really, he's had to grow up a lot. His older brother has, too. All of us have had to grow up quite a bit, I guess, with this experience, but he's been really remarkable.

I know this is going to sound odd, but we tried to make cancer fun. He's a kid. He's a child who wants to play and goof around, be out with his brothers and sisters and have fun. So we made cancer as fun as we possibly could. We played Navy SEALs in the children's hospital. We'd say, "Clear the elevator," and the boys would jump in. We did this commando jumping all over the place. We would crawl through the cafeteria with people in it. We didn't care who was there. We'd peek around the corner and we'd peek around poles. We became well known throughout the hospital. We'd be in a big, huge lobby area and hear some nurse or doctor yell across the hospital, "Navy SEAL, get down!" and we'd all hit the deck and army-crawl across the floor. And over his bed we put up a tent with glow-in-the-dark stars on the ceiling so that he could see the

stars with what vision he had. We made that our summer camping experience. People came from other parts of the hospital,
and this was not a little hospital, just to see our tent. Then we
had Congressional Medal of Honor recipients who came up
and visited Garrett. But the "Navy SEALs, get down!" was the
best. We have friends who are Navy SEALs, who most likely
have some kind of post-traumatic stress disorder, that said, "You
know, that's not an appropriate game to play." And I'd say, "Just
relax, pal. He's going through his own war right now." And it
went on from there. We had Doctor Rubber Gloves. When the
doctor wasn't there, I'd put on the rubber gloves and just tickle
the daylights out of him. We didn't want to make it any more
miserable than it already was. And I think he came out on the
other side of it better off.

A critical aspect that parents don't think about is what one
child's illness is doing to the other kids in the family. We have
four kids. Our youngest two were two and three when Garrett
was diagnosed, and frankly, it didn't affect them as much. They
were too young to really understand what was going on. But
Garrett's older brother was seven when Garrett was diagnosed.
He understood very clearly what was going on and that his
brother and best friend could die. The impact on him was as
great as it was for my wife and me. And so we found other children who had mothers or fathers or brothers or sisters with cancer, others his age that he could talk to, or maybe a bit older
who could be a mentor to him. We were also very careful that
any special treatment that was given to Garrett included Ryan
in some way. There wasn't a TV or newspaper interview, a
picture, a gift, or anything else that was given to Garrett that
wasn't also given to his brother. We've continued that through
to this day, because we can't have a child jealous of a disease.
And I think that our thoughts and our stance on that have been
to Ryan's benefit. I think we were wise in that respect. We did
that from Day One. Even when we were in the midst of our

confusion, we always made sure that taking care of Ryan and the other kids was a priority as well.

Cancer's a roller-coaster. It's all about emotion. In 1970, child-hood cancer was a death sentence. We were real fortunate that we were diagnosed in the year 2000. Seventy percent of childhood-cancer patients today survive. There is that other 30 percent, though, so that's something that we still have to deal with. Garrett's not out of the woods completely.

Having a child with cancer doesn't feel like the natural order of things. When your child's looking at death, it just seems wrong. You know, I'm supposed to die first and they're sup-posed to mourn me. It's not supposed to be the other way around. It's difficult for everybody, and the way some of my friends have reacted has been frustrating for me as well. We have friends who, to this day, will not talk about it, have never approached the subject, don't ask about Garrett and never have, and these are close friends. I don't know if I did something that made them angry or if they're just uncomfortable. It's very dif-ficult to understand how other people react, and it took us a while to realize that this is just the way that they're dealing with it. They don't understand it and they can't deal with it, so they would just rather avoid us. There are friends that we've lost, who we just don't talk to now, and it's not for any other reason than that they're uncomfortable. I've tried to approach some of them, and of course they deny it because they don't want to seem shallow. But it's not that they're shallow, it's just that it's difficult for them. With childhood cancer, the order of the world is all screwed up. The timeline isn't supposed to be kids getting sick and dying. That confuses a lot of people. Then there are other people who just can't shut up. They feel like they have to say something profound or they have to carry your pain in one sentence when they would have been better off just saying, "I'm so sorry." And sometimes you want to smack them but you can't, so you just hug them and let the comments roll off your back.

Survivorship is not just surviving; it's living.

I'm Eric Miller. My family and I are three-year cancer survivors. My son Garrett is a three-year brain-cancer survivor.
We're living strong.

"Life is a journey. It's not a guided tour."

MIKE**KRIZ**

I was diagnosed in August of '97 with carcinoma of the left breast, so I'm a male breast-cancer survivor.

We were on vacation in Vail, Colorado, and after skiing I was in a hot tub and just happened to graze my left nipple and there was a lump. It was about the size of a BB, or perhaps a small pea. I was thirty-six years old and I had essentially blown everything off that was ever health-related. I'd never had any health complications. My wife is an operating-room nurse. I'm in the health-care profession as well. She was persistent that I seek out some kind of opinion on this, so I went to a family practitioner. I had never even gone to a doctor before. They ordered a sonogram, which came back inconclusive, which was then followed up with a mammogram, which proved negative.

My neighbor was a plastic surgeon, and later during that summer I was out cutting my grass. I had noticed that the lump had gotten considerably larger, and I pointed it out to my neighbor and he said, "By all means, let's just stop by the office and we'll yank that thing out." So a couple of weeks later, he did a very gross excision of this little lump. It was about the size of a small strawberry, about two centimeters by two centimeters. And in the midst of this he said, "Hey, Mike, I've got news for you." I said, "What's that?" He said, "This isn't cancer." I said, "It's not?" He said, "No, this isn't cancer at all." Luckily he had the foresight to send it off to pathology. Several days later, he came back and told me the news that forever changed my life. I had Stage-III breast cancer.

Everything changes in this business as they continue to do research and look for different therapies and different modes of treatment. What they did to me at that point was immediately treat me with a high dose of chemotherapy. Three months after that, they did a radical mastectomy, so my left breast is gone. After that, I went through a stem-cell therapy program, which is kind of a bone-marrow type of a transplant program. First they gave me yet another ultra-high dose of chemotherapy. Then they gave me back my stem cells so that I could rebuild my immune system and help my body heal from the shock it received from the truckload of chemo. And after that, the doctors followed up with radiation therapy. So I had been a young, healthy individual, and they essentially threw everything that was possible at me. That was almost six years ago.

My therapy was very aggressive. I think you always have choices, but at that time it was thought that with the high-dose chemotherapy and the stem-cell replacement therapy, they could kill the cancer that was left in my body after surgical removal of my left breast. They thought that there were cancer cells throughout my lymphatic system, and in other parts of my body, that were undetectable by CT scans and other tests. So the thought was to go after it as aggressively as possible. That was the trend at that time, though not exactly the way they would treat me today. Today they probably would not treat me as aggressively.

Since then, I have not had a recurrence. I haven't had a scan since sometime in '97. Immediately after I completed all my treatment protocols, I began having scans every three months. They would do a quick examination and look for a breast-tumor marker through a blood test. Then I went every six months for that same battery of tests, and now I go once a year. So that's kind of where I am right now. I'm on a yearly follow-up protocol.

Physically, I feel very good. I don't think that I really endured any major physical detriments. I think that my energy is probably where it was previously. The chemotherapy kind of shocked my reproductive system, so I'm infertile. My wife and I would have liked to have had another child, but when I entered my treatment regimen, things went very, very quickly and I was never really given any options in terms of being able to bank any of my sperm. Our heads were spinning at such an incredible rate that by the time we figured out what was going on, we were a little bit too late on that. I think that those discussions should be standard protocol between the patient and his treatment team of doctors and clinicians. In all other aspects, however, I've been able to maintain a normal lifestyle for myself. In terms of the physical well-being of who I am, I have definitely returned to who I've always been.

I've got an indentation and a six- or seven-inch scar across the upper left portion of my chest. It really doesn't bother me. When I first completed all of my therapies, I consulted with my plastic-surgeon friend, who had been involved from the beginning. I thought that I would go in for a nipple reconstruction. He did some stuff that really didn't work, and after that I decided that it wasn't a major cosmetic issue for me. It's a small thing.

When you're thirty-six, full of vitality and working in corporate America, you worry about 401k plans and things like that. Concerns about my health were very far away from my mind. Today, I try to live life from kind of an adventurous side of the equation. I try to be much more cognizant of humanity, of who we all are. Cancer is a great equalizer. When you have cancer, it doesn't really matter if you're Hindu, if you're Jewish, if you're Christian, Muslim, if you're from America, from Germany, or from the Middle East. It's an equalizer that makes you want to be much more open to all of humanity.

Initial diagnosis is incredibly traumatic. You bargain with

God a little bit at first: "If I can get just two or three more years out of this thing and see my child reach the age of five, then I'll be happy." But those pleas are always there. There are no guarantees in my treatment. So we just move forward one step at a time and one day at a time.

There is a fearful gratefulness. I don't claim that I've beaten anything here. I think "survivor" is a very appropriate term. I'm a cancer survivor. I guess you try to find a better place in life for yourself and try to come back and somehow give back to the community and the people who helped you. You try to be a part of something that can help people who might be afflicted in the future. Sometimes I do feel a little bit guilty about things. I feel guilty about my own survivorship when I know of people who did not survive, people who helped me survive my illness who are not here today. That's a hard feeling to live with. And then I sometimes feel guilty that I'm not doing enough to help, even though sometimes I just want to get away from it, move away and do something else to get away from it. There is a range of emotions.

I do feel that I have a debt to pay. I'm here, and there is a higher order in terms of what God wants me to do with my life. Why am I here when others aren't? What's my place? Careers are great, but it's a very shallow life if that's your sole existence. There's much, much more to this whole thing than jobs and money. So I want to be able to give back and do some different things.

I had a very good support system. My wife worked at the hospital where I received my treatment, so we had some insight and some advantages in terms of being able to pick and choose where we were going for treatment and what we were going to do. I owe a tremendous debt to my wife overall. Dealing with family is unique for every person. There are survivors who never wanted their children to know about their illness. For me, that wasn't the right way to deal with it. I wanted to be open and very up-front with my kids. I knew that I was going to be bombarded with chemotherapy; I knew that my hair was going to fall out; I knew that all of these things were going to happen. So I wanted to confront them and speak to them openly about it.

Cancer has been a very big part of my children's early lives. One of their grandfathers has passed away from cancer in the last couple of years. Then I survived breast cancer, and now my father has pancreatic cancer. He was diagnosed about four weeks ago. So this is something that affects all of us in varying degrees and in various stages of life. And unfortunately for my children, it's there. They know that all too well.

In my last follow-up, my new physician asked me about doing some genetic testing and some genetic mapping. I'm still trying to determine whether or not this is something that I want to do. I clearly see the benefits associated with it in terms of my immediate lineage. But we live in a very crazy administrative-health-care environment in which there can be some very negative ramifications. For example, my children, if they carry a positive gene for cancer, might have trouble qualifying for health care in this country, should their results be shared with insurance companies. There are some very, very difficult questions associated with the issue. So I'm still trying to figure out exactly what I want to do with that, if that information can be protected, and those kinds of things. It's a scary reality associated with some of the genetic markers and genetic testing that's available out there. It's a weird decision that you really should not have to make based on those criteria, but you've got to think about it. That's where we are today.

One of the things that you realize when you go through something like this is how precious health-care coverage is. I had excellent coverage. I worked for good people. I maintained my function as a sales manager and conducted my business and my corporate duties very well. From that perspective, I was most fortunate. At that time, my wife's father was a multiple-myeloma patient as a senior citizen on a fixed income. He lost his battle a little over two and a half years ago or so. What I didn't realize is that seniors did not have a prescription-drug plan. I just thought that we provided that for them, but apparently we don't. This was even before the last round of major elections, when health care became such a big issue. You develop a different level of compassion for what people go through, not only from the physical ailment of a disease, but what they have to go through to fight through the system to get care in a compassionate manner. It's bizarre to think that we're the world leader in health care when not everyone has access to it. I don't think that health care should be considered a privilege. It should be a right for all of us.

There are different levels of hope as you go through the cancer experience. When you first hear the words, "You have cancer," it's incredibly devastating. But then when the doctor says, "But I can cure you," you hang on to those four letters, "cure," and that gives you so much incredible hope. Hope kind of puts you on a path. I saw that path, and there was a goal at the end, and hope was taking me there. My dad's cancer is totally different from what I have been surviving. When you get into the survival rates and percentages, he's in a tough spot. But he's doing well, and he has hope and a chance at a cure. He takes his piece of hope and he goes forward with it every day. Once you get through the battery of tests and they've diagnosed your cancer and stage, what's left is hope. That's what you play with every day. Then you wake up one morning and you realize that you're alive. You wake up and you hear and you smell and you taste and realize, "Man, I'm alive."

I read a T-shirt that said: LIFE'S A JOURNEY. IT'S NOT A GUIDED TOUR. And that's exactly what it is. It's a journey. I don't sweat the small stuff. If I'm stuck in a little bit of traffic and I'm running fifteen minutes late for an appointment, it's not a big deal. I'm going to get there. I don't want it to sound like I take a completely nonchalant outlook as to who I am or to life or to my career or any of those kinds of things. I mean, I'm an upstanding citizen and I want to do the right things, I want to produce for my company and all of those kinds of things, but I just approach it a little bit differently. I just have a different awareness about it.

I've always been a relatively confident and optimistic person. I'm not a doom-and-gloom kind of guy by nature. But inside, I'm still worried. There is a world of uncertainty out there. But I can try my best to transcend that uncertainty with hope and optimism. There will always be things that I can't control, so I have to just deal with them and move on.

I think survivorship gives you a chance to do some different things with your life. You're on a totally different pathway than you were before cancer. For me, survivorship means hopefully being able to give something back to the community, give something back that benefits all of humanity. Survivorship has given me the chance to do things that I've wanted to do, go places that I've wanted to go. I never would have experienced this journey if it hadn't been for cancer. I never would have run a half-marathon at ten thousand feet in Crested Butte, Colorado. There are many other things that I want to do, and when it's all over and done, I want to be very satisfied with who I was and the way that I lived my life.

My name is Mike Kriz, I am forty-two years of age, and I am a six-year breast-cancer survivor.

Live strong.

"I can't ruin today worrying about tomorrow."

LORI**MONROE**

I became a survivor on September 18, 2001, when I was diagnosed with Stage-IV lung cancer.

At the time I was diagnosed, I considered myself a very healthy person. I had gone in for a hysterectomy. They did a chest X-ray for the surgery and came back saying I had some infiltrates in my lung. Nobody really thought much about it. We thought it was nothing. They gave me some IV antibiotics and we followed it up two weeks post-op. When the infiltrates hadn't cleared, we went on with a bronchioscopy. When the bronc came back showing that I had cancer cells in my lungs, it was a complete shock. Nobody expected lung cancer. I didn't have any symptoms at all. I wasn't short of breath. I didn't have a cough. I didn't feel bad. The month before, I had spent three weeks in the Tetons and in Yellowstone hiking at elevations of 14,000 feet, and I wasn't short of breath. I was very healthy. So the diagnosis was a complete shock.

At that time, I was concerned, but I wasn't devastated. I thought, "Okay, well, we've caught this cancer early." I'm a nurse, so I felt like I knew how to get through the medical system. But as the hours and days went on, I realized I knew nothing about lung cancer and nothing about navigating through the medical system. We did some scans, and they told me at first that I had cancer everywhere. They told me I had cancer in the cervical spine, in the clavicles, in the lymph nodes around my neck, the lymph nodes around my aorta, my adrenal glands and liver, and that there was really very little that anybody could do. They gave me six to eight months.

When I went to see the oncologist, I got the biggest shock of all. She said my choice wasn't going to be *which* treatment we chose, but even *if* we started treatment at all. She said that right now I was feeling good and that if she gave me chemotherapy, it would do horrible things to my body and I'd be unable to take care of my children. But I just wasn't willing to sit back and do nothing. I went online and started searching for information about lung cancer. I sent e-mails off to physicians all across the country saying, "I'm forty-two years old. This is what's going on. This is what I've been told. Who do you suggest I go see?" A lot of the replies came back saying that I should go to the same hospital. So I made an appointment there. It was very, very difficult to tell my children. They were ten and thirteen at the time. It was one of the hardest things of the entire cancer experience. I had to tell them that we had this cancer to deal with and what was about to happen. The only thing I knew to do was just be honest with them. I told them that I would tell them everything I knew as I found it out, that they would never have to wonder. I don't know if that was the right or the wrong way to approach it, but that's what I did.

When I went to the hospital, they repeated all the scans. What they told me was that they weren't sure that the cancer was as advanced as I had first been told, though they still thought it was Stage IV. There was a physician here in town who said that he wasn't as concerned about the other cancer, the cancer in the other places, as he was about the cancer in the right lung, even though I'd already been told that the right was okay. What he wanted to do was go in and take out a piece of the right lung to see if it had as much cancer in it as the left lung did. I agreed to do that procedure. It's called a thoracoscopy. And when I woke up from that surgery, I felt to see if he had done a mediastinoscopy and he had not, which meant that the

cancer was in the right lung and was still Stage IV. When he
came in and told me that it was still Stage IV, he also told me
that there weren't any other surgeries that he could do. He
could not remove the cancer that was in the left lung. Again,
we were devastated. We didn't know what to do until later that
same day, when he called and told me that he would do the surgery anyway. He said he'd been thinking about it, and that if I
still wanted him to do it, he would go ahead and do it. And that
was the first time that I had any hope in the three weeks since
the diagnosis. So we scheduled the surgery for a left lobectomy
and went through that surgery a couple days later.

After that surgery, I took two months off and just recovered.
And that's when I met my doctor. My first two oncologists
hadn't been very hopeful. Both of them said that there really
wasn't an option for surgery. They had both told me to just do
the chemotherapy, take my six months and that was it. That was
all they could offer me. When I met my doctor, he told me that
there wasn't a cure for the kind of cancer I had. But what we
would try to do was keep it from growing, keep it from metas-
tasizing for the next twenty years. I said, "Okay, well, I can live
with that." It was wonderful to be able to have that hope.

I feel very strongly about the quality of care in clinical trials.
I think the care with the trials is somewhat better than it would
be if I was just seeing a general oncologist and getting standard
care. For me, the clinical trial was a very positive experience.
They watched me so closely. Everything was monitored. Some
of my medications were even paid for by the company that was
running the trial. I just really felt like I got better care. I had a
nurse practitioner who monitored everything and was there to
answer every little question I had. When I was first diagnosed
and looking at all the options, talking to various oncologists
throughout the country, I was very surprised at the number of
doctors who advised me not to go on a clinical trial. They said,
"They'll make a guinea pig out of you," or, "Don't let them try
to do this to you," or other things. But for me, standard care
wasn't very promising. Chemotherapy in lung cancer works for

only 6 percent of the patients. So I figured what they were using now that was already approved obviously wasn't very effective. I might as well try something that hadn't been approved
yet and boost my chances. What I took was an epidermal
growth factor inhibitor. I did a year of chemotherapy in a trial
for Taxol-carboplatin, an experimental drug combination. And
for lung cancer, that's worked very well. I did very well on that.
The cancer remained stable the entire time.

But in October of that next year, the drug company that was
supplying the drug thought that maybe the cancer was starting
to grow again, and they wanted to discontinue giving me the
drug. I got frantic. I started calling their medical director and
found out that the half-life of this drug was only three to four
days, and without the drug, the cancer would start to grow
again. But my doctor never felt like the cancer was growing.
He thought that it was stable. We reread the CT scans, and he
continued to assert that the scans were stable. But still the company thought it was growing. It ended up taking eight weeks of
going back and forth before they finally said I could go back on
my meds. By this time, however, I had gotten too panicked and
had called some other surgeons around the country. I spoke to
one wonderful doctor in particular. She asked me to send her
my scans, which she looked at, and said, "If your surgeon will
do it, do another surgery and get it taken out," which is what
we did. We did another thoracotomy in December of 2002, this
time on the right side. After that, I was cancer free with no evidence of disease for sixteen months . . . until last April. Then I
had another recurrence. This time it was in the upper left lobe,
and I couldn't find a clinical trial that really fit my cancer.

Most of the clinical trials right now use some form of an epidermal growth factor inhibitor. Unfortunately, what I'm finding now is that the new clinical trials are written with a prior
epidermal growth factor inhibitor exclusion, so I can't get in.
I've tried to talk with some of the medical directors of the drug
companies about why they write their trials like this. And they

say "Well, if you've already failed an epidermal growth factor inhibitor, we don't necessarily want you in our trial." But I never failed my treatment. It worked. So not being able to get into a trial because of exclusions has been a bit frustrating. It seems like it's a double-edged sword. I think the drug companies write the trials for their benefit, and if the patient gets any benefit out of it, it's kind of a sideline bonus. So we did yet another surgery. This would be my fourth lung surgery.

All the surgeries to my lungs have taken a good bit of the lung tissue out. I probably have only 40 percent of my left lung left and 80 percent of my right. Not only are thoracotomy surgeries very, very difficult, and very painful, but they're also short-term in terms of treating cancer. You know, you recover from the surgery, you recover from the pain. But you don't always recover from cancer.

I don't feel short of breath when I'm just doing routine everyday things. If I'm hiking in the mountains, though, I do. After my first two surgeries, I went to Colorado to snow-ski while on chemo—partly, I think to prove that I could still do it. And again, after this last surgery, after my fourth thoracotomy, when I got out of the hospital, I stayed home two weeks and then I went back to Colorado and still was able to get up to 14,000 feet. I was short of breath climbing uphill, but I did it, I can still do it.

I do have some pain from this last surgery that is still kind of unresolved. It's a lasting chronic pain that we're working on. I've gone to see a chiropractor, and I'm going to make an appointment with a pain specialist. I have also started working out with a personal trainer, doing yoga and lifting weights three or four times a week. I'm also going to look into acupuncture, because I think it might help, too. I'm going to try anything that I can. I think that if I mix alternative medicine with conventional medicine, I can come up with the best solution to alleviate the pain. And I think that for a good bit, I can do things to help myself. I think exercise and staying active is a way to get around that, get things back to working normally. I still have too much pain, but hopefully we will get that resolved.

I often feel fatigued. I don't know whether it's from the lack of lung tissue or whether it's just from the long treatments or even something else. The fatigue on chemo was like no other fatigue I've ever felt. It's not tiredness. It is an overwhelming to-the-core fatigue. The fatigue after surgery is also different than the fatigue after chemo. Fatigue after surgery is just more of a draining. It's hard to get motivated again. It's hard to push forward. I've never had radiation, but I've heard that the fatigue from that is also horrible. I don't think I have the same stamina now that I had before the treatment, but I don't necessarily think it's from the cancer. I think it's from the treatments. I'm always pleased on days when I have more energy than my daughters. But most days, I just kind of have to realize and accept that I don't. I have this fatigue, and I have to plan for it. I try not to schedule too many activities for myself in one week. Even though I went through the chemotherapy for five months and then the trial meds for nearly a year, I never missed anything I wanted to do with my daughters. I still went on all their school trips. I attended all their games and activities. I just planned for it. I can remember there was a period of time right when I was diagnosed when my thirteen-year-old had activities every night. I told her, "Emily, we can't do this. I can't keep up with you. I can't take you all these places. We're going to have to pick and choose. We'll do activities two nights a week." And then she reminded me that I'm not the only one going through cancer and that she needed her friends. She needed to be away from it sometimes. She was right. So I just changed my day. I arranged it so I would lie down and take a rest before school was out so I'd be ready to go on and do the activities with the kids later in the evening. You just have to plan. You have to realize what you're capable of doing, and then plan. If you know what to expect, and you don't try to fight it too hard, you can carry on a somewhat normal life.

There are a lot of things you learn from having cancer. It's kind of bad that you have to have a disease like this to learn so much. I wish that I could have learned the things I know now without having to go through it. There's a popular song now about living your life as if it was the last day, you know. And I think that's really true. Everybody knows that you never know how many tomorrows you have left. But it changes you somehow when you are actually being told that you have something that you're probably going to die from. It changes the way you look at things. It changes the way you approach things. It changes the way you feel about everything. And those are not bad changes. Cancer is not good, but sometimes the things that evolve from it can be very positive.

When I was first diagnosed and just beginning to learn about lung cancer, it was terrifying. I would go online and look at the statistics. Even if you combined all the stages, from the earliest stage to the most advanced stage, the survival rate is extremely low. The stage that I have, Stage IV, has 0 percent survivability. So statistically, it's terrifying. During the very first month after diagnosis, I could only read this stuff online for twenty minutes before I would say, "Okay, I can't read anymore," and I would sign off. But then I realized that they are only statistics. They are only numbers that were compiled from data at least two years old. And I'm not a statistic. No matter how many statistics they throw at me, I'm an individual, and they can't predict what's going to happen to me. The statistics tell what's *likely* to happen to a group of people, not what *is* going to happen to an individual. Then I began to find people who actually had Stage-IV lung cancer and who had been alive longer than zero years. They had already surpassed the life expectancy of six to eight months. Obviously the stats are not correct in my case or those other individuals' cases.

I have always been concerned about recurrence. It's Stage-IV lung cancer, which they tell you there's no cure for. So a recurrence is likely at some point in the future. I don't think I'll ever get used to going in for scans. I felt so healthy when I was diagnosed that it was just so unbelievable to me that I was as sick as I was. After that, I have not yet been able to trust my body again. When scan day comes, I get really anxious and tense. It's all I can think about. For sixteen months there was no evidence of disease, and then it was April when I was diagnosed this year with cancer again. I swear I could almost tell by the doctor's footsteps walking down the hallway that what he had to say wasn't good. When he rounded the corner and I saw his face, I knew right away. I just said, "Well, where is it? Have you already looked at it?" And he told me yes, that he had, and that there were some new spots. We had to battle it again. But as long as battling it gives me more time, that's kind of what it's all about anyway. We all have a certain amount of time in life whether we have cancer or not. As long as I still feel good and still want to fight, that's what I plan to do. I just deal with it as the days come. People have said to me, "Learn to live one day at a time." At the time, I thought, "Well, everybody only lives one day at a time. I don't know anyone that lives two at one time," you know. But having cancer, I've come to understand that from a new perspective. I have learned to cherish and enjoy this day for what it is. I try to enjoy the time I have, even on bad days. And if there's a recurrence, then I'll deal with it then. But I can't ruin today worrying about tomorrow.

Having that realization made me reevaluate and prioritize the things that are important to me. And one of those things is speaking out about cancer. But spending time with my children is also very important. So I don't put off vacations or any other time with the kids. I try to keep cancer out of the spotlight so it's not the focus at home. I don't like to talk on the phone to other patients when my kids are around. I don't want them to hear the word "cancer" all the time. I try to balance things out. Supporting other patients is very important, but really my family comes first, and I spend the majority of my time with my girls.

————

After the first surgery and before I started chemo, I had a lot of time to sit back and think about things. I thought about treatment and what I was going to have to do to make sure I stuck around for a while. And what I came up with is that you have to assault the cancer from three different angles. One of those angles includes the medical community and conventional medicine: the doctors, nurses, surgery, chemotherapy, and radiation. Whatever options they throw at me, I want to be able to do and use them to the fullest extent. And if I need to get second opinions, if I need to go somewhere else for treatment, if I need to advocate for my own treatment, then I will have taken full advantage of modern medicine. But I don't think that you can rely solely on the doctors and medical community. You also have to see what you can do for yourself, which includes eating right, getting adequate rest, getting exercise, and generally taking care of yourself. You have to build up your strength, increase your own immunities, and make yourself as strong as you can so that your body can fight the cancer. The third thing in my arsenal against cancer is my faith in God and the power of prayer. That is as equal a part of my treatment as medicine and a healthy lifestyle are. There are no statistics on what the power of prayer can do, and there's no way to measure what faith in God will do for the spirit. But I feel strongly that there have to be equal parts of all these fighting mechanisms in order to beat or live with cancer. So if you surround the cancer with those three things, then I think that your chances of fighting it are much better.

It was both heartbreaking and beautiful to watch what faith has done for my children and how they have grown, how they have matured, and how their faith has strengthened through all of this. They're awesome girls. They have been very, very supportive. We all just kind of rallied around one another. I was actually married when I began my fight with cancer. I was married for nineteen years and found out that he didn't "do" cancer. Now both of my daughters think that I can do anything. And right now, that's okay that they think so. I don't think that

that's a bad place for them to be. I think that it will get ugly soon enough and that everybody should just enjoy what we have today.

I've really had to plan for the future. I don't know how people who don't know how to research things, write letters, and read all the fine print on the insurance policies manage. My life insurance has tried to cancel me three times and once came very close to canceling my entire policy. I got help and got that stopped. But they would love not to insure me right now. As far as health insurance goes, I have to return to work to maintain my group health insurance. I'm considered uninsurable right now, so I've got full disability from Social Security, which makes me eligible for Medicare. But I don't like my options for health-care with Medicare. So I need to get group health insurance. I need to go back to work to do that. I am still hoping that my employer has a job for me. After my first surgeries, I took two and a half years off and then went back to work and went right back into my same job. They were great. This time around, I've been off about three months. I'm still hoping that they have my job when I go back. If they don't, I'm not quite sure what I'm going to do. Somehow I'll manage.

I had never considered myself at risk for lung cancer. I assumed that people with lung cancer were, you know, seventy-five-year-old men who'd smoked two packs a day. But when I started reading up on the statistics for lung cancer, it was just very, very frightening—terrifying, really. There are 174,000 people diagnosed with lung cancer every year. And I feel like they probably have the same feelings that I did on their diagnosis: that it's a hopeless situation. So talking to them and letting them know that it's not necessarily a death sentence is very important to me. It's a way to give back to the people who helped me. We have very few lung-cancer advocates, in part because we have very few survivors. But there's something else that I'll throw in here now. There's a negative stigma attached to lung cancer: that somehow the patients have caused their own illness. Every time that I tell somebody that I have lung cancer, they ask, "Well, did you smoke?" It's as if they're really asking, "Well, did you cause your own disease? Did you get what you deserved?" I don't think that they mean it that harshly, but that's what it sounds like when they ask the question. What I have read about lung cancer is that many patients don't even seek treatment because they feel that they caused their own disease. They feel that they smoked and then got what they deserved. So they don't ask for help. I often wonder whether if we could change our statistics, patients would seek better treatments; if they would demand better treatment. But a lot of them feel shame and guilt about having lung cancer. I don't know that there's such a sense of shame for other cancer groups. I don't really even know of another disease in which the patients are actually blamed, not even HIV anymore. But with lung cancer, there are some very strong assumptions attached. A surprisingly large percentage of lung-cancer cases diagnosed will be in patients who have never, ever smoked or who quit smoking ten years before. I went to the World Lung Cancer Meeting in Vancouver, and there was a fellow there from the UK who actually said, "You know, we shouldn't even be treating Stage-IV lung-cancer patients," meaning that they are simply the ones who aren't dead yet. His whole philosophy was, why waste our chemo drugs and expensive pharmaceuticals on patients that are dying anyway? And he didn't even want to treat them. Hearing that was all very shocking.

It really angered me when people tried to predict my death. My thinking was that the doctors couldn't predict my death from cancer any more accurately than they could predict my death from getting hit by a car on my way home. You can't do that to somebody. I think a message needs to be sent to the medical community, including the doctors, to watch what they say to patients and how they say it. I went through three oncologists before I found my doctor, who has been hopeful and creative in treating me from the beginning. And none of them were very optimistic. Every one of them tried to tell me that I probably wouldn't be alive in a year. I think that no matter what degree you have, whether it's an M.D. or a high school diploma, you never have the right to take the hope away from another human being. Hope is essential to life. Healthy people that have nothing wrong with them have to have hope of getting through the day, or they don't get out of bed. And I think physicians, oncologists in particular, need to be very careful about how they speak to their patients. As a cancer patient, you cling to every word they say. And it made me angry that they would try to predict my death and tell me that what I had wasn't even worth treating.

Survivorship to me means just living with the disease. I have considered myself a survivor since the day that I was diagnosed. I am still here. I'm still surviving. I'm still living.

I'm Lori Monroe, I'm forty-five, and I'm a three-year Stage-IV lung-cancer survivor.

Live strong.

"You have to be the CEO of your own care."

GREG**FERRIS**

I became a cancer survivor on December 29, 1999, when I was diagnosed with CML, chronic myelogenous leukemia

The biggest physical issue I have to deal with is an ongoing one. It has to do with the fact that before I was diagnosed I was a young, healthy, twenty-seven-year-old male who worked out constantly and was in good all-around shape. And with treatment and the drugs that I've been taking for the last four years, I haven't been able to be that person. So the two biggest physical issues are the effects of the chemo destroying my body and then the post-treatment side effects caused by the drugs that I'm still on. Prednisone, in particular, has a really deleterious effect on the body, on the bones, on muscle structure, on everything, even the psyche. So the medication side effects in conjunction with just not feeling well in general from the leukemia make the entire process of trying to get well very difficult.

It's hard to say exactly what it means when I don't feel good. It means different things on different days. As a result of the bone-marrow transplant and the prednisone, I have a lot of muscle aches as well as chronic sinusitis. And I often feel fatigued and icky. My head's clogged and it just doesn't go away. No matter what I do, it doesn't go away. Every day, I sort of wake up and do a check of my body and say, "What's bothering me today?" And every day it's something slightly different. Sometimes my stomach hurts because I haven't eaten, or my muscles are achy, or my head hurts, or I'm just incredibly fatigued, or irritable. All sorts of things. And so I do a check every morning to see what I'm going to deal with today. The struggle is to try to persevere and overcome whatever obstacles present themselves during the day and make the most of the day in spite of them.

I think one of the biggest difficulties that I face, and that others with a chronic illness face, is trying not to be a hypochondriac while still being incredibly sensitive to what your body is telling you. It's a very, very difficult balancing act, because you don't want to constantly be calling your doctor and saying, "I had this pain in my knee," or, "I had this pain in my stomach. What does that mean? Do I need to come in?" But at the same time, you're constantly told to be hypervigilant. It's difficult. But after four years, and I have by no means perfected it by any stretch, I've learned how to walk that hypochondria line pretty well. When a symptom comes up, if it stays around for a while, I call my doctor, or if it's a different sensation than I've ever felt in the past, I'll send him an e-mail or give him a call. But if it's something that I can recognize, then I'll deal with it myself.

I guess "treatment" means different things for different people. I would definitely say I'm still in treatment. But treatment doesn't mean chemotherapy to me. I've had two finite treatment periods. First there was the chemotherapy leading up to the bone-marrow transplant, followed by the transplant itself and the first hundred days of acute care post-transplant, which included a hospital stay of thirty days. I was receiving chemo throughout that time. So that was the first definite cancer treatment. But since then, I've continued to be treated for the effects and the side effects of the transplant, specifically that of graft-versus-host disease.

Graft-versus-host disease is quite simple. It occurs in the bodies of people who've received transplants from other peo-

ple. There are many people who receive transplants from themselves, so graft-versus-host is not an issue. The disease is basically the graft's immune system viewing my body as foreign. It's
doing what an immune system does. It sees things that are foreign to its body and attacks them. So the new immune system
that I have, which came from my sister, looks around my body
and says, "Wait a second, this isn't Greg's sister's body," and it
starts attacking me. Oftentimes the disease burns itself out after
there's been a period of time for the host and the graft to sort
of get to know each other a little bit better and find equilib-
rium. But in many cases that doesn't happen, and the new immune system requires medication to keep it from attacking the
body. Obviously my sister is getting back at me for all the things
I did to her as a child. I'm still coping with that after almost four
years out of surgery. Graft-versus-host requires me to be on
heavy immunosuppressants, including prednisone. Not only is
my immune system being suppressed by drugs, it's also weaker
just because it's not my original immune system but rather that
of another person altogether.

Consequently, hygiene becomes incredibly important. Being
careful about being exposed to people who are sick is incredibly important, especially because I have a suppressed immune
system from the graft-versus-host disease. I'm at a higher risk of
getting sick than the average person. As a result, before every
action I take throughout the day, I go through a series of checks
and balances. I have to assess whether the risk is worth the reward. The simple act of shaking somebody's hand is actually a
danger to me. The biggest transfer of germs is through the
hands, so I'm constantly fighting against social constructs and
social norms that we take for granted. Is it okay to drink out of
somebody else's glass? Is it okay to shake hands? Is it okay that
people are constantly putting their hands up against their nose
and shaking my hand or patting me on the back? I'm constantly
washing my hands and carrying around antibacterial stuff. I
have to think about every single decision I make. If I go to the

movies and somebody two rows behind me is coughing, do I get up and move, or do I stay? Making that decision can preoccupy me for a half-hour. How bad is that person coughing? Do I even go to the movies? Do I go at an off time?

Individually, each little decision is probably not that risky, but in the aggregate, living a normal life is an incredibly risky proposition for me. There's a balance between the reward and getting sick. I've done things and then gotten sick, which has made me pull back and say, "Well, I'm going to be more careful." But that doesn't work for me, because then I'm not experiencing life. So then I go out again and probably get sick again, and then pull back again. There's a constant back and forth and give and take. It's emotionally draining and difficult, but it's the constant seeking of the reward, of living, of living life. That's the point of all of this. I mean, why go through everything that I've gone through if life isn't worth it? And life is definitely worth it.

Being a cancer survivor is just life. My life is not any different than anybody else's in a lot of ways. This is just my particular journey, my particular experience. One thing that I know I have had difficulty with, and I've discussed this with friends, both patients and non-patients, is the challenge of defining who I am. *Do* I redefine myself? And is there a redefinition of relationships and interactions? Some people have treated me differently. You know, there were people who were sort of ancillary friends and all of a sudden they embraced me and said, "Oh, my god, you've been through this," and they think that, for whatever reason, since I've been through this, now I have some insight into the world or some greater knowledge. I don't. And then other people treat me the same way they always did and never mention cancer. But then it's the big white elephant in the room. Addressing the cancer is a difficult issue, because even if you ignore it, it is still there and it still changes things. But at the same time, it doesn't change things. It's hard to explain. I'm still the same person in many ways, but I'm also not. I look different. I feel different. I think a little differently. But you know what? Even after four years without cancer I would look different, feel different, think differently.

At the time I was diagnosed, fertility was not something that was first and foremost in the discussions, and that is something that I really resent. Hopefully that is changing. I know that there's been a big push to make fertility a much more up-front issue for both men and women. But it was much more, "Let's get you straight on chemo, right away," and no real discussion like, "Wait a second, before we do that, let's think about the future and what effects there might be down the road." Fortunately, my family was very involved and asked important questions, and I was able to store some sperm before the chemo started, but not as much as if I had really been put on the correct regimen. Fertility is definitely an issue that needs to be discussed at the beginning, from diagnosis on.

What I found is that the doctors don't tell you a lot of things, which is both good and bad, I guess. For instance, I was told prior to the transplant, "Give us a year, and we'll give you back your life. In a year, you will lead a life indistinguishable from the life you were leading before." That's a pretty powerful statement and one that shouldn't have been made, because that became my expectation. But on the other hand, if I had been told everything that was going to happen to me prior to the transplant, I don't know if I still would have done it, quite frankly. I mean, I probably would have, but I would have thought a lot longer and a lot harder. In any event, I think there's a good reason why doctors sometimes don't give you the full story. But I think a lot of times, they don't give you enough of the story. What I have found is that you have to be incredibly aggressive, stubborn, and even obnoxious at times, because there's nobody out there who cares about your life more than you do. And if you think that somebody does, and you don't want to be pushy or you don't want to say something wrong, you're the one who is ultimately going to suffer the consequences.

I've experienced that firsthand, where I've suffered consequences because I didn't ask, "Well, what about this? What about that?" I didn't know that if I had a cold that I could then get graft-versus-host disease of the lungs. But that's what happened. And I wasn't told that. Was I not told that on purpose? No, of course not. But again, it's this complicated balancing act of trying to get as much information as possible and understanding all the implications of the disease and the treatment as much as you can, while at the same time trying to keep your sanity. You're not a doctor. I'm not a doctor. Rely on the medical training of the doctors, and go ahead and live your life. But at the same time, be aware of the consequences, good or bad, of any decision.

I think having access to information is incredibly important. At first, I regularly studied my blood counts and looked at all the information in my charts and files. Eventually, I got to a point where I didn't really want to do that anymore. I knew that if there was a problem, I was going to be informed, and that to be hyper-focused on all the minutiae of what was going on in my body was actually detrimental to me, because it wasn't allowing me to live. At the same time, having the power to access that detailed information at any time is incredibly important. Having the knowledge and the confidence to step up and say, "Wait a second, this isn't right," or, "I'm not feeling well like this. Can I see my file? Can I make sure?" Because people make mistakes all the time. It's unfortunate, but a lot of the responsibility comes down to you, which is tough. Not only are you fighting the disease and fighting to regain and retain normalcy in life, but you're also fighting the bureaucracy. But you must fight to make sure that you're getting the care that you need. Fight to make sure that you're being treated with respect. It's a constant battle that gets really tiring, but there's really no other choice. At the end of the day, you have to be the CEO of your own care.

There are definitely emotional issues associated with having cancer as a young adult. There are emotional issues associated with having cancer, period, but I think there are issues unique to young adults with cancer. As a healthy young adult, you feel invincible. You feel like you have your whole life ahead of you and all your energy is spent planning for the future and working toward building a foundation for the rest of your life. I was twenty-seven when I was diagnosed. I was single and living in New York City and planning for the rest of my life. I felt like my whole life was laid out in front of me. I didn't expect something like this to come into my life. It changed my whole perspective. I don't look the same as I used to. And the prednisone, the chemo, the effects of the treatment completely changed what I could and couldn't do in the world. I had been living a life where I was working and playing hard and doing all the things that I wanted to be doing. Granted, I didn't have everything figured out by any stretch of the imagination, but I was on a path. I turned thirty a year ago, along with a lot my friends. And at thirty, everybody sort of takes stock of their life. Where did I expect to be when I was thirty? What did I expect to have? I thought I was going to be married. I was going to have a kid. I was going to have a house. I was going to have this job. Very rarely does that actually play out the way you think it's going to or the way you thought it would when you were twenty-one. So all of my friends were sort of going through this reevaluation of, "Wow, where am I in life, and what is it that I want?" I was going through that, too, but I also had all of this other stuff on top of that, like am I even going to be around? What is my life going to be like? Am I going to be able to function normally? And what is "normal" anymore?

I have to worry about being sick, about getting sick, and about the implications of that. But how do you conduct a normal relationship when you're concerned about catching a cold from somebody? How do you deal with that? Do you only date people who've had cancer, too? How do you bring it up to somebody who hasn't? How do you help them understand? Is it fair to them to show up on a first date with seventeen bags of luggage saying, "Here are all my issues. Want to have dinner?" Is it fair to them to say, "Yeah, I'm a good guy, but, you know, Bob over there is a good guy, too, and he hasn't had a bone-marrow transplant. Why not go out with him?" I think that there are a ton of issues associated with being a young adult, having your life ahead of you, having it all change, and then trying to deal with how those changes are going to impact your life while still retaining the hope and desires that you had before. How do you actually make those things come to pass, given the new constructs of the reality associated with having cancer or having had cancer?

Cancer is a very individual thing. Anyone who says to you, "This is what cancer means," isn't telling you the truth, because cancer means something different to each person. To one person, cancer can mean salvation, a second chance, a blessing. To another, it can be a curse. And I think that the bond that ties all of us together is our desire to persevere and get beyond it. That desire can manifest itself in several ways. Some people just want to deal with their disease and get it over with without ever talking or thinking about it again. And you know what? That is absolutely fine, because that's what works for them. Other people just want to talk about it and talk about it and give back and give back, and that's equally great, because without that giving back and without that support, without that activism, the whole field of research wouldn't move forward as quickly as it is. The point is that the meaning of cancer is very individualized and very personal. Whatever works for each person is really all that matters, as long as the drive and desire to survive and persevere are there. To live strong. That's really what it's all about.

I think hope is what drives us all. Hope is definitely what drives me. Without hope, what do you have?

My name is Greg Ferris, I'm thirty-one years old, and I'm fighting leukemia.

Live strong.

"I am not a statistic."

KAREN**SEECHE**

My name is Karen Seeche. I became an ovarian-cancer survivor when I was diagnosed in February of 2000, and I became a breast-cancer survivor when I was diagnosed in September of 2003.

One of the problems with ovarian cancer is that the symptoms are very vague and are often confused with other symptoms. For about a year before I was diagnosed, I had a lot of gastrointestinal ailments. I would wake up in the morning belching or constipated. And when I would go to my doctor and complain, I was told, "Well, you're menopausal." "You have an underactive thyroid." "You work full-time. You take care of your sick mother. You've got to calm down." That went on for quite a while. I had a checkup with my gynecologist in November of 1999, and he couldn't find anything, either. But a couple of months later, I got to the point where I literally could not button my pants anymore. So I went back to my endocrinologist. And this time, I said to him, "There's something wrong with me. I can't button my pants, and I know I haven't been eating that much." This time, when he did an internal exam, he felt a tumor and sent me for a vaginal ultrasound, which showed that I had tumor activity. I was called right back to his office. I had come from the gym that morning, where I had walked several miles and done about a hundred crunches, and I was on my way to be with my mother, who was dying of esophageal cancer, when my own doctor sat me down and said, "You're not going anywhere. Please call your husband. I've got to talk to the two of you." So my husband Steve came over and my doctor looked at us and said, "I am pretty sure that you have ovarian cancer." And then, because I think he's someone who deals mostly in endocrinology and younger women with fertility problems, he sort of just blurted out, "And you've got about two years." Steve and I were just so blown out of the water. I mean, how do you go on from there? I was a very healthy person. I had just moved to Boston, I was renovating my house, and I'd just moved my mother into a retirement home when she became ill with esophageal cancer.

I couldn't believe it. He told me that I had to go in for surgery right away. And I said, "I can't go in for surgery. My mother is dying." But he insisted. So that's what happened. He booked me for surgery within ten days. Thank God I never had to tell my mother anything. She died in peace thinking she had three well children. She died, I buried her on a Friday, and I went in for cancer surgery on Monday. I was really out of it when I had the surgery, between grief for my mother and grief for losing my health. For somebody like me who's a very high-energy gal, this was very, very difficult to accept.

I come from a family with a history of breast cancer. Consequently, I was always expecting that I'd get it. My mother was diagnosed with breast cancer at sixty-nine and died of her second cancer, esophageal cancer. My grandmother died at thirty-eight and my aunt at forty-four of breast cancer. So I was pretty much expecting cancer, but I figured that I'd be like my mother and I would be all right. And by then, I thought, by the time I'm sixty-nine, breast cancer will probably be a non-issue. But no one had ever discussed ovarian cancer with me. I find it especially appalling since, after my mother was diagnosed with breast cancer, my sister and I were followed very closely by a major Boston medical center. No one discussed ovarian cancer with either one of us. Of course, there's much more awareness now than there was even five years ago. But very often, in families with histories of breast cancer, there is also ovarian cancer. I had asked my mother years earlier, "What did your great-grandmother die from?" And, typical of that generation, my mother had said, "I don't know. It was something between the neck and the knees. I don't know what it was." People often didn't survive ovarian cancer for any length of time. So perhaps she really didn't know of anybody who had had ovarian cancer. But as far as a medical diagnosis goes, I feel that I fell through every crack there was to fall through with the ovarian cancer. And so I was diagnosed Stage IV. Certainly, I could have been diagnosed Stage I had anybody really said, "My god, this gal comes from a family with a major history of breast cancer. She's complaining about these G.I. symptoms. Send her for a vaginal ultrasound soon." My doctors weren't tuned in to my situation. And I think that's the reason I want to speak out, so that women will be more aggressive with their doctors, especially women with family histories like mine. I feel to some degree that it was unnecessary to be diagnosed at Stage IV the way I was.

Once I was finally diagnosed, I was very fortunate. I had extensive surgery where they took out everything that they could. I had already had my uterus removed when I was thirty-eight. They also did an exploratory and removed as much tumor as they could. I was pretty filled with it, because I was diagnosed Stage IV. After surgery, I went into chemotherapy. The gold standard is considered to be carboplatin and Taxol. My doctor was involved with a clinical trial, where he was adding another drug, gemcitabine, which had been used in lung-cancer treatment. I said I wanted to participate in the trial. I wanted the big guns. I had no fears about it at all. I just knew that I wanted the most aggressive treatment available.

I went into that clinical trial, and I did lose my hair. I went the wig route once or twice but got rid of it, 'cause I couldn't stand it. I wore a baseball cap and I did just fine. Very often, in a Stage-IV diagnosis, they can't remove everything when they do the debulking surgery, so I was left with a small amount of tumor. What I'm the most grateful for is that despite the fact that I have Stage IV, I'm a survivor of four and a half years. I'm grateful that I do react to chemotherapy. I have a fabulous brother-in-law who's a neurologist, who said to me on Day One, "Don't listen to statistics, because you're not a statistic. I see patients in my office every day who are supposed to be dead. Don't get caught up in it and don't think of yourself like that. Just keep your eyes straight ahead, stay focused, do what you need to do. And the chemotherapy is everything." I think he is right in many respects, because, unfortunately, I have seen women who were diagnosed with far less cancer than I have who are not alive today. Why I'm still here and they're not, I don't know, except that I react well to chemotherapy. I don't stay in remission very long. But when I do wander out of remission, I wander just a little bit, and then my doctor puts me on something else. I'm on a drug now called Doxil, which I have done very, very well with and ironically is also used for breast cancer. So given that I did have that very small bout with breast cancer, I'm sort of being treated for both. I'm very grateful to be alive and to be here. I hope that women who read this will think about themselves in terms of both of these cancers and go to their doctors and be aggressive. I only wished I had known more about ovarian cancer, because I would have pushed my doctors more.

I found out that I had breast cancer when I went in for a routine mammogram. My doctor called me and said, "I think you might possibly have a small breast cancer." And one-two-three, he got me in immediately for a biopsy. It was a very small, what they call DCIS, ductal carcinoma in situ, which is a very small breast cancer in the duct. They removed that with a lumpectomy. Nothing had spread to the nodes. Had I had a tumor that had been estrogen-positive, I would have been put on tamoxifen, but my tumor was not estrogen-positive. They couldn't give me tamoxifen, and I could not have radiation, because I'm

on the Doxil. So what I do now is just go for frequent mammograms and checkups and continue on the Doxil. I don't
mean to sound flip, but the breast cancer is sort of like a "P.S."
to the whole situation. I'm essentially an ovarian-cancer patient
who has had a little breast cancer on the side. But when you
have this genetic predisposition, it's essentially the same disease.

Because I'd had my uterus removed, I never really knew when
I was menopausal. I did have a little bit of the hot flashes and
what-not, but essentially, nothing really bothers me. If I get a
little hot flash, I open a window. I just live my life and do what
I have to do. I'm very fortunate that I have that kind of dispo-
sition. People bring to cancer what they bring to everything in
their lives, whether it's their marriage or a job or family or relationships with friends. I think the same type of coping mechanisms and personality traits used every day are necessary when
fighting cancer. I used to see women in my support group who
were very, very angry. I didn't really understand how someone
could be angry at a parent who might have passed down a gene,
when the parent suffered from it as well. I do understand being
angry that you have something that somebody else doesn't
have, but I guess I just feel that if you've got something, you
have to move forward. Do the most you can for yourself. I just
pray to God my kids don't have this, and that if they do have
this genetic mutation, that science will be advanced enough that
this will not be a serious thing for them. But I don't think anger
helps any kind of situation.

I could be angry about what happened the summer before
my mother died. I had driven her from her retirement home
up to a major Boston hospital for genetic testing. And I got a
call months later in November that they hadn't had enough
blood to run all of the tests, and that I needed to bring her back
in. I was in the middle of moving and my mother was already
not feeling great in this retirement home. And I said, "I can't
bring her back in. My mother is not well. She just can't do anymore." So the genetic testing was a failure because they wanted

to test my mother first, because she was the known cancer risk. They should have started with my sister and me. So nothing ended up happening. The whole thing was kind of forgotten. I got so busy with my mother and so busy with my move. But then I was diagnosed, and my mother died, and my brother-in-law, the doctor, said to me, "Karen, whatever happened with that genetic testing?" He was really furious when I told him what happened, and he called up the fellow at this hospital, whom he knew from a residency program years ago, and said, "Where is my mother-in-law's blood?" And the guy replied that they had it, but they didn't have enough to run the two tests, the BRCA 1 and BRCA 2. And my brother-in-law said, "For God's sake, run the BRCA 1. You've really let this family down." Sure enough, we get the call back. My sister and I go over to the hospital. And I'm sitting there with all these stitches, having just been diagnosed with ovarian cancer. Sure enough, my mother did have the BRCA 1 mutation. Yet another crack that I fell through . . . It's really a shame, because when I took my mother that day to do the testing, she kept saying, "I'm doing this for my girls. I'm doing this for them." After that, my sister went for testing. Thankfully, she does not have the BRCA mutation.

I have no problem telling people I'm a survivor. It's very interesting, because my mother and father were very secretive about cancer. My dad had two cancers and died from his second one. He had prostate and melanoma. And my mother had breast and then esophageal cancer. They were wonderful role models for me, because I saw how they lived with cancer, not just how they died from cancer. They lived very well with cancer, even though they didn't talk about it. But I tell people about my experience, because I think that maybe people can learn from it. If I could just get one other woman to see her doctor and maybe push her doctor a little more than I pushed my doctors, then I want to tell them.

The best thing about having cancer is surviving it. And I

think when people look at me and when they hear me and they see me with energy and looking great and feeling great, they say, "I don't want to stay home if I feel a lump in my breast. I don't want to stay home if I feel bloated and I'm constipated and I don't feel well." They won't be afraid. My aunt died from fear. My mother always said to me that by the time her sister told her that she felt a lump in her breast, it was already too late. By then, it had spread to her lungs. She was afraid to tell even her own sister. Afraid to tell her own husband. It's the fear that can kill you more than anything. So telling people I'm a survivor is really important. Does anybody want to belong to the cancer club? No. This is the club nobody wants to belong to. But having ended up in it, I feel that I should do whatever I can to make something good out of this, to try to help somebody.

I have chronic recurrent ovarian cancer. So if I can live the way I live and be on the kind of medication that I'm on and get the kind of results that I have, then you know what? I'm happy to be chronic. I am happy to be chronic. My prayer is to be able to stay chronic and wait for better medications that hopefully will come along. Meanwhile, I'm very active in the National Ovarian Cancer Coalition. I am very active in our local wellness community, which was founded by Gilda Radner. After my mother passed away, we started a fund in her memory for women with cancer, which sponsors lectures and support groups on breast and ovarian cancer. I tutor less-fortunate kids. I take a course at the Museum of Fine Arts. And my husband's going to bed before I do, because I'm up doing laundry and I'm on the phone with friends.

Survivorship means that I wake up every day. I put two feet on the ground. I enjoy my day. I do what I feel is important to me. I'm with the people I love. What could be better? That's what it is. In life, we're all playing for time. It's just that cancer pushes its progression right in your face. People who don't live with a chronic disease have this sort of unlimited feeling about time, kind of the way you feel when you're an adolescent and you've got the top down on your convertible and the radio blaring. You think you're never going to die and that things will always be great like this. So that's really what surviving is. That you just have a little more sense of life and its finiteness. None of us knows what's going to happen. We all wake up every day and hope for the best for ourselves and our families and our kids.

My name is Karen Seeche, and I'm a four-year breast and ovarian cancer survivor.

Live strong.

"Changed for the better."

JOSEPH**NIPPER**

My name is Joseph Nipper. I'm thirty years old. When I was twenty-one, I was diagnosed with squamous-cell carcinoma of the major carotid gland. And, yeah, it changed my life . . . for the better overall, I would say.

My surgery was thirteen and a half hours long. They basically cut my ear completely off. They cut from above the ear all the way down into the shoulder. They took out all the soft material, all the muscles, all the bits of everything in that area out. It's called a full right radical neck. And they weren't kidding. It was a very radical procedure. They ended up taking my ear canal, the eleventh thoracic nerve. They resected a piece of my facial nerve out of my ankle. Obviously there were major pain issues. For six to eight weeks, every single day I was in the worst pain of my life. It felt like the side of my face was going to explode. But after those weeks of pain, I began to go to physical therapy. I had to learn how to move my body again, now that I had these new issues.

If I were to give one piece of advice to anyone about to undergo a full radical, it would be to ask for the good drugs. If you've gotten to the point that they're going to do a full radical on your neck, there's very little that you can do besides cope. It's a very serious operation. You know, the doctors give you this form that outlines what's going to be wrong with you when you wake up. You have to look at that form and then sign it before they'll actually do the procedure. And you start to read off these things—Okay, I'm going to be deaf, I'm going to be paralyzed, I'm going to be . . . It's like, wait a second, I have to sign this and approve this? I have to approve what you're about to do to me? It's very, very hard, very hard mentally to sign that piece of paper and go into the surgery knowing what you've just been told.

I was a pretty aggressive patient. I really wanted to know exactly what was going on. I wanted to know why certain things were necessary; why I was doing all of this. The funny thing I found is that no matter how many questions I had, they didn't have answers to a lot of them. The doctors know what they know, but they don't know everything. I think that's one of the failings on our part as patients. We put so much faith in the members of the medical community. We expect them to have all the answers. And when they don't, they just give us this, "I'm sorry. We can't do anything about that," and we're left with that and nothing else. I dealt with that uncertainty by praying. I got spiritual. I put a lot of faith in God instead of the doctor.

My life did a one-eighty and changed for the better. Back when I was twenty-one, I was a pretty crazy kid. I was having a lot of fun, but also getting in a lot of trouble. I don't think I knew what was truly important in life. So when I was put through this gauntlet, I emerged on the other side having learned what is truly important and what life is really about. It was an amazing transition. I was headed down the wrong path, but after going through the worst experience of my life, I found that there was a better path, and that it was no problem to stay on it. A lot of that change is a result of what I went through, but I think it was even more a result of the people I met and talked to throughout the whole experience. They explained to me what was important in life and how I should change my perspective toward what was truly important. I'm amazed. I think the only reason I'm such an amazing person today is because I was put through the hell of cancer at such a young age.

My philosophies and outlook changed drastically. A lot of it was a result of things that other people gave me, bits of their own wisdom. Really important little tidbits of how to face the world. When I first came out of surgery, I was pretty seriously affected by it; my face and smile were gone. One really good friend told me, "Joseph, anybody who cares how you look doesn't matter." Coming to grips with that was big for me. It was total transcendence from the depth of despair that I had been in. I woke up from surgery and looked in the mirror at the side of my head. To say that I looked like Quasimodo would be giving me a compliment. The other thing I learned is that life is what you live. So once you kind of get away from the therapy and the surgery and you're starting to recover and feel better, your ability to live life is determined by you alone. And everything starts expanding from there—your whole life is in front of you.

I am now much more a person who values what's truly important, as opposed to the material things in life, like what people look like. I began to look deeper. I found a deeper meaning and a deeper value to everything.

Right after the surgery, I had to deal with learning how to talk again. That was one of the hardest challenges for me. But it wasn't until I was in that seventh or eighth week of radiation that my mind actually started changing. I realized that I wasn't thinking the same way that I used to. I didn't have the energy to think much at all. Trying to step out of that gray cloud that my head was in, slowly coming back into feeling normal and eating and thinking, was bizarre. I mean, even thoughts like, "Maybe I should go to the bathroom now." Or, "Maybe I should watch TV," became difficult decisions. The radiation grays everything out. It grayed out my taste buds. It grayed out my ability to pay attention to a conversation. So many of my senses and abilities were just no longer there. I got out of the habit of taking a shower every day. I got out of the habit of brushing my teeth and hair every day. I just didn't have the energy. It wasn't until weeks after the radiation that all that stuff started coming back. I started to build up energy again, started taking care of myself and taking care of my body, started thinking about those kinds of things. But it took weeks and months before everything returned to normal. It wasn't just a matter of starting to do all those things again though. I literally had to relearn how to brush my hair. I had to relearn how to brush my teeth; how to move my hand to make the brush move. And it's exhausting to have to focus so much on such a simple thing at least once a day.

I don't have nearly the long-term memory that I did before treatment. A lot of it, going all the way back to my childhood, is still kind of grayed out. It's hard to recall a lot of the bits and pieces. I still get flashes of memories, but it's nowhere near the recall level that I used to have. Also a lot of the information that I used to know about computers and networks and how they work just isn't there anymore. That obviously affects my job.

Having cancer affected my ability to work. At the time, it put me completely out of work. When I went through cancer at twenty-one, I was a freight-dock loader. So I was working out on a freight dock throwing forty-five-pound boxes all night. After I went through surgery and radiation, I couldn't throw a thirty-pound box, let alone a forty-five-pound box. I had to quit. I'm a permanently disabled member of the Teamsters Union. So after that I went back to school, learned computers, got my degree, and took off in a different direction. That's been part of my one-hundred-eighty-degree turn.

The hardest thing for me emotionally was feeling like I had to deal with this by myself. I had broken up with my girlfriend at the time and had kind of stopped talking to all my friends. I just wanted to huddle up in a corner and be by myself, be alone. I was so afraid of everything. I mean, walking into it was like, what have I done to myself? And the doctors had no explanations as to why I got cancer. They only had figures and charts and statistics. I was lost emotionally. I didn't know what to feel, so I kind of chose not to feel at all. I tried to just bury all of it. And, you know, that had its own recourse, because it certainly came out later. But at the beginning I was pretty dark emotionally. I just tried to hide it all. After the fact, people came up to me and said, "Oh, Joseph, what happened to you? We can't believe this happened. Why didn't you tell us?" It was then that I learned what true friends are. I learned who the true friends were who would come around and help me out. They really cared about me and they wanted to see me do better. So I really wish I would have done it differently, because there were a lot of people who did really care for me. I had just shut them out thinking I was doing them a favor. But in retrospect and with hindsight, I found out that I had kind of denied them and denied myself the chance to feel that sorrow as it was coming and let it go.

The hardest thing for me with my friends was working out how to communicate my feelings. How do I communicate these feelings of fear that I'm going to die? Regardless of how you do it, the point is that you just need to. You have to let all that go. You have to let go of all your conscious thoughts about how weird it's going to be for them, and just appreciate the fact that these are your friends who do care about you and want to hear what you have to say. They want to work through it with you. I separated myself, broke away, and ended up going through a lot of extra pain because I was doing it by myself; whereas if I would have plugged into my own friends, plugged into their network, I would have felt a lot differently and had a lot more support. Although it seems sometimes that it would be a lot easier to go through something like this by yourself instead of with your friends and family, it's not. It's always going to be easier with people around you who love and care about you. They will support you and tell you that they care about you, and you'll be able to feed off that support.

As far as my parents were concerned, I didn't tell them much and kept them in the dark. The hardest part of this cancer was that nobody could figure out why I had it. There was no explanation for it. And so I felt like it must have been heaven smiting me or something like that. I thought it must have been some kind of a personal judgment . . . either from me on myself or from God on me. So, I didn't want my parents to be tangled up in it. I didn't want them to have to go through all the craziness and fear and pain that I was going through. And it was only after talking to them after the fact that I realized they were going through their own painful struggle, too. We just weren't going through it together. We weren't gaining the support mechanism out of it, even though we were all going through just as much pain. Unfortunately, that was something that we realized later. Of course you have the option to keep your family in the dark, but they are going to be your best source of support if you let them in.

Your family cares so much about you, and they are, of course, going through a similar experience, mourning a sibling or a son or daughter. In the nine years since I had cancer, I've had kids and become a parent. If they were to be injured or diagnosed with cancer, well, that's one of the scariest things I can imagine. It must have been so hard for my parents when I was sick. I know when my therapy began, it was truly a rollercoaster. Getting radiation every day made it hard to get out of bed in the morning. I needed the support of somebody bringing me a plate with food on it—though it didn't do any good, because I had no taste buds. Everything tasted like cardboard. My parents did as much as they could. I would advise parents and family members who want to get involved and want to support their loved ones to talk to them and work with them to find out what they feel comfortable with. Maybe the patient refuses help from his parents because he'd be more comfortable accepting help from a friend. Perhaps it's somebody who the patient really likes and respects. Sometimes a non–family member can have a more profound influence in getting the patient to open up emotionally. It can be embarrassing to spill your pain, especially with a close family member. But someone who's a little bit more detached from the family, somebody who's slightly outside, just a friend who the patient respects, can offer an objective ear. I think that's what finally allowed me to break out emotionally. Different friends of the family would come and talk to me just to ask how I was doing, if I needed anything. It was a friend who said the thing about it not mattering how I look to others who truly cared about me. If my parents, instead of my friend, had said the same thing, I probably wouldn't have accepted it.

That being said, friends and family should keep trying to reach out to the patient. Attitude and emotions change every single day. One day I wouldn't want to talk to anybody, and the next day I wouldn't let them leave my room. They just need you to be there. Fill them with good energy and lots of love. It's all you can do. The patient also gives the caregiver support in that they are responsive, they're thankful and appreciative of that care. It is easy for caregivers to lose hope, because the patient often doesn't have enough hope for themselves, let alone for others. So they kind of have to sponge off the family member's hope. They kind of have to suck it in and take in all the little bitty bits they can get. You can't go all the way down through the pain and come to hope. That doesn't happen. Hope comes from the outside. Hope comes from other people and being able to share that pain and knowing that it's okay and that tomorrow is going to be another day.

I don't worry about recurrence, because, you know, if it happens, it happens. It'll just be another stride I'll take in the race. I went through it once and I lived. Go through it again? Well, then I'll have to deal with it a second time. Hopefully, I'll live again. I can't be afraid of it. I can't be worried about it, because that's just going to slow down everything else in my life.

These days I can walk into any social situation, get right in the center of it and not be nervous at all . . . until I remember, "Oh, wow, the side of my face is kind of hanging limp, and I wonder if anybody is noticing my teeth." Sometimes I feel like I can do anything in the world because I've gone through this amazing life-and-death experience. I've come out on the other side, feeling like the Incredible Hulk. "Oh, I can do anything now. I've made it through the worst depths and the worst pits. Everything else from now on is going to be easy." But then there's always that insecurity of how I'm going to be perceived. We live in a society that is organized by rules and social expectations. Whenever you kind of run your head into those rules, by becoming disfigured for example, it's like an Incredible Hulk running into a brick wall. You get a big mess and people don't know how to react.

I constantly remind myself about the support I get from my family and friends. I have so many friends now and my life is more about enjoying them, enjoying those relationships with friends, as opposed to worrying about how they are going to perceive me. You know, it's true that your real friends don't have any different perception of you just because the side of your face is limp or because your teeth are messed up or because you've got a huge scar. They don't care about that. They are your friends. They like you however you come.

I had several different doctors. I had a facial specialist. I had an oncologist. I had a nerve resection guy and several other specialists. So when they all got their bills totaled up and insurance subtracted its covered amount, these guys still wanted *a lot* of money. I think that was one of the biggest bombs that fell on me. I had just assumed that insurance would cover everything. Of course I wanted the best help. I wanted the best nerve guy in Dallas. I wanted the best face guy in Dallas. I wanted the best because this was me. This was my face! And then they dropped the bomb, the twenty-five-thousand-dollar bomb. And it's like, "What?! What? I don't have that much money." It was a rough experience that I had to work through with my family. We eventually got the doctors to kind of meet us halfway, which they didn't like doing.

All those bills made me wonder if having "the best" was really worth it. Well, while I finally came to terms with my friends about not caring how I look, I thought about everybody else in the world. My face is going to be with me at every job interview. It's going to pass every person I pass on the sidewalk for the rest of my life. The better medical care I got and the better the surgeon I had practicing the latest techniques, the more likely it was I'd be put back together to resemble as closely as possible the person I was before I got sick. But the long-term financial result of that was that that better surgeon wasn't covered by insurance. I could have been paying for years. I guess you have to decide: What is the value of how you look? It depends on who you are. I mean, for a network administrator, it's not such a big deal. But, you know, if I was a politician or something, I might have made a different decision.

When I was done completely with therapy, I was kind of lucky, because I had a place to go. I had been a volunteer for several years down at a folk festival, so I got a job down there. It was camping, so I had a place to stay. There were thousands and thousands of friends who truly cared about me. When they saw me, they were just blown away. They took one look at me and said, "Oh, my God. What happened? What happened? What can we do for you? Do you need a massage? Do you need somebody to stand here and just talk to you for a while?" I was given the most amazing and powerful support from the people at that festival. There was so much love and so many people worried about me, telling me how great I was and how great I looked. Even if they were lying, it made me feel better. And I think that kind of helped ease the transition from going through therapy into normal everyday life. Three weeks of getting massaged every day and being hugged and loved and told how great I looked was enough to rebuild my spirit. By the time I left the festival that summer, I was a different person. I was filled with power and ready to go back and do whatever needed to be done. And I think that's when I got most serious about college.

I had already been to college. I had lasted only a couple of years and partied my way out the door. But it was only after going through cancer and then getting better that I was able to turn my sights back toward college and look at it with a more intent focus. Now I had an idea of why I was there and what direction I wanted my life to take.

The word "survivorship" means learning to live. When I found out I had cancer, I thought I was going to die. My granddad had had cancer a couple of years before, and he died within a couple of weeks of diagnosis. I was diagnosed and immediately thought I was going to die. And then the strangest thing happened after surgery. I woke up, and all of a sudden, I had to deal with being alive. I had prepared for death. I had prepared for being buried. I had prepared for leaving this world. I hadn't prepared for life. I had to wake up, and I had to get out of bed, and I had to go on. And that's what survivorship means—getting out of bed and going on with life.

My name is Joseph Nipper, and I'm a nine-year cancer survivor. Live strong.

"I wish I would have asked."

OCTAVIO**ZAVALA**

My name is Octavio Zavala and I became a survivor on October 5, 1984, when I was diagnosed with acute lymphoblastic leukemia.

When I was first diagnosed, things were so confusing and so scary that I didn't know exactly what was happening for the first few weeks. I didn't even know that leukemia was cancer until about a month after I was diagnosed, when I read about it in a book. In hindsight, I think that if I had to go back and do this all over again, I would ask my doctors and nurses a lot of very specific questions. What is leukemia? Why did it happen? And what is going on in my body? Chemo sounds complicated. It sounds like it's going to be a long three years. Why? What is the stuff, and what can it do for me now and later? Back then I was a little bit embarrassed about things like puberty. I had turned twelve, and I was already starting to look at the girls and check them out. I wanted to hang out with them and start dating and stuff. I was already kind of a short kid. But being on chemo, I knew that there was no way, having no hair, being and looking so sick, that that was going to happen. That made me want to ask my doctor when, if ever, those side effects would go away. Would I eventually look better so that the girls would like me? Would I start puberty with everybody else? But for a twelve-year-old, these were embarrassing questions that I was afraid to ask. Gradually, as things happened, my questions were answered. But I wish I would have asked anyway, just to ease my mind a little bit. I realized, after finishing the three years of chemo, that the nurses and the doctors were people that I could have trusted with these questions. I would encourage anyone not to worry about being ashamed of things, and to ask the most personal, intimate questions you might have if you trust your doctors and nurses.

I think parents understand that, especially during the teenage years, it's hard for children to ask their parents personal questions. Parents are grownups but they were once teenagers, and they can understand that despite the struggle and the focus on getting cured and overcoming the chemo side effects, a teenager needs as much as possible to think about "normal" teen things. Parents should know that even though you may not be comfortable asking them directly, they can encourage you to ask others, people who aren't your family or close to you, but people who you do trust and who you feel a little more comfortable asking these questions of. If they know this early on in the chaos, it's really going to help you a lot.

My parents did try to get me back into school as often as I was able to go. It was one of most important things for me psychosocially. At the time, it was a pain in the butt that they made me go back, but now I know why they were doing it. I missed almost all of my seventh-grade year, much of my eighth-grade year, and a lot of my ninth- and tenth-grade years. But that was one of the few ways they were able to give my life some normalcy. It didn't completely solve the whole patient-isolation thing, and I still lacked some social skills, but it did help me to hold on to remnants of a normal life throughout this very tough time.

Academically, the schools were very accommodating. The hospital also had a great in-hospital teaching program. They were really good at coordinating at-home schooling until I was medically able to go back to school. I still was behind, but not as behind as I might have been, given my diagnosis and treatment.

Socially, it was a whole other story. I wasn't socially back to normal until a good five or six years after treatment, when I started college. College was like a trial by fire. It's an environment where independence, resourcefulness, and social skills are vital. I didn't have any of those because of the treatment and the isolation. So college, a sink-or-swim environment, was where I had to hurry and catch up with my peers in order to survive and make it and graduate.

There was a teen-impact program at the hospital that began about one year after I finished treatment. I wish it had been around when I was there. It was started in 1988 and was set up to help bring together teens who have or have had cancer. I work for the program now. We help them share their stories, but also help them develop and maintain social skills by interacting with other teens in an environment that's safe, where people won't be judged for not having hair, for not having a limb, for not having the best social skills. They all understand. I think it's important for teens now, even though their focus might be on living and coping with treatment, to really think about what they want for the future. They should interact regularly with peers, both patients and non-patients. They need to maintain whatever social skills they had before getting sick because they will have a life well beyond this cancer experience. And life beyond cancer is very important.

Not having hair for over three years was very hard. My hair fell out within a month of treatment, and it stayed out for the entire three years and four months. That was really difficult because, again, I wanted so badly for the girls to like me and to go on dates with them. But I felt like there was no way that anybody was going to date a scrawny, sickly-looking kid with no hair. Few teenagers know of a teenager with cancer or even know what a teenager with cancer looks like. I had friends who sympathized and supported me, but I still felt that nobody wanted to date me, and that really sucked. Also, my friends played football and baseball, and even though sports was never a natural interest of mine, I wanted to play, too. But there was just no way that I could; the chemo was so physically draining. It just sucked all the energy out of me, and I spent more time in bed and more time throwing up than I did out on the field. That was frustrating.

It's really easy, just due to the physicalness of cancer and its treatment, to put yourself in the hands of others and let everybody take care of everything, even worrying, for you. You let somebody else worry because it's just so hard; it takes so much energy just to continue, let alone think and plan for yourself. But that's a very dangerous habit to fall into. I fell into it, and I think other teens fall into it, too. As hard as it might seem sometimes to cope physically and get through it, you really need to stay in control of your life during treatment as much as possible. You need to be able and allowed to worry about things. You need to know as many details about your cancer and care as you can, even though you think you might not want to know. You might just want them to do their thing and leave you alone. But take it from me: It's really important for you to know the details and be in control of your treatment. Your parents, out of instinct, are probably going to want to protect you and take care of everything for you. Understand their intentions and appreciate why they're doing things, but also gently resist it, because that's not good for you, either. Just remember that there is life after chemo. No matter how poor your prognosis might be, you need to maintain hope. Hope is something that, though you may have taken it for granted before you were diagnosed, you will need in order to focus on life beyond cancer. I didn't do a lot of these things, and so for ten to twelve years after chemo I had to make up for lost time. I had to take back the control over my life that I had given up during my treatment.

I'm not a parent yet, though one day I hope to be. In my line of work, I see what parents go through when they're told that their child has cancer. Most parents describe it as an instant death sentence for both the child and for them. Then it seems natural for parents to be overprotective, to shield their child from any worry, from any harm, to give the child extra-special treatment, to expect the siblings to understand why all the focus is on the sick sibling, and to think that they know everything that's best for the patient, who is young and really doesn't know what his or her needs are. But none of this is wholly true. I think the best thing a parent can do for their son or daughter is allow them to have as much control over their treatment decisions and over their life as possible, no matter how hard it might be to let go of some of that control. At the very least, parents should help their child believe that they have some control. They need to understand that even though their natural instinct is to put all of their time and energy and focus on the sick child, it will benefit them and the child more if the focus and attention can be spread on the rest of the family. Too many parents neglect their own needs, and that can be very dangerous for the whole family, including the patient. Especially in the case of leukemia, where treatment is three or four years long, parents neglecting themselves and the rest of the family can become a routine and a habit that's going to be really hard to break once treatment is done. Beyond that, it is important to have optimism, no matter what kind of statistics or prognosis are given. If a parent doesn't believe their child is going to make it, then he or she probably won't believe it, either. Everyone needs to believe that, no matter what they are told.

As wonderful and necessary as it is to have great doctors and nurses, they are only on the cancer side of your life, and you do not want the cancer side to be the only side of your life. Don't let your whole support system be made up of only your doctors and your nurses. When you're done with your chemo and no longer see them every day, you are going to need others to be there. So it's really important to have strong support from family and friends. I was lucky that I did have that support. I think that's why, even though I struggled psychosocially after chemo, I ended up being all right. Those people were there then, and they have been there for me ever since. I've seen a lot of other survivors who didn't have that support and have struggled for many more years after their treatment. Be honest with yourself, and if you feel that you don't have a strong support system right now, find one. You can make one.

The fear of recurrence was pretty strong right after chemo. But as most people would expect, it tends to diminish over time. A lot of survivors go through periods when we completely ignore the past illness and maybe even engage in some reckless behavior, almost as if to say, "I'm going to show you, cancer, that you're irrelevant in my life." But I think at some point you come full-circle and incorporate your cancer experience into the rest of your life. You don't ignore or deny it, but it's not the center of your life or your primary fear anymore. It's just something that's there and has become a healthy part of your life and history. I do, from time to time, worry about recurrence, but I've been off treatment for almost twenty years. I'm a different person now. I've done so many things in these twenty years. I've gone to school, I've had my heart broken and have broken some hearts, I've worked different jobs. I'm a different person. Heaven forbid I walk into the doctor's office tomorrow and am told, "You've got acute lymphoblastic leukemia." But if that were the case, I would treat it as a completely new diagnosis, because twenty years later I'm a completely different person. I think my fear of recurrence has become like my fear of walking out in the street and being hit by a car. It's just one of the many possible ways I can die. But it's healthier for me not to dwell on it.

Compared to other people my age who have not been through cancer, I really love and value life. But I fear death, too. Even though I consider myself a religious person, a person of faith, I do still have fear. But despite that fear, I love life and try to appreciate it as much as possible. I don't want to miss any opportunities. I think my philosophy is that life, even when it gives you really bad times, is worth living. The bad times are actually opportunities if you can be mentally healthy going into them.

While I was sick, my approach to living, which was both good and bad, was to go day by day. I would think, "What do I need to do to make it through this day as comfortably as possible?" That approach worked because it helped me weather a lot of the harshness of the chemo. But it was bad in that I only focused on each day and not on the future and life after chemo. In retrospect, I might have done things differently. I would have taken things day by day, but also made a point every day to think about life and the future.

Survivorship means a lot of different things to me. It means eventually transitioning out of the patient-survivor role and into the healthy, productive, adult-survivor role. An adult survivor is someone who has properly incorporated his cancer experience into the rest of his life. For me to say I'm a survivor, I have to be doing just that. I *was* a patient; I'm *now* a survivor. My experience is part of my life. It's a medal of honor that I wear and something that I can teach my family and friends about. I am an advocate. That is what being a survivor means to me.

My name is Octavio Zavala and I'm a nineteen-year leukemia survivor.

Viva fuerte.

"Attitude."

DAVID**DRIVER**

In February of 1999, the doctors diagnosed me with pancreatic cancer.

Prior to diagnosis, I had had some digestive problems, which they attributed to what they thought might be gallstones irritating the pancreas. They had planned on going in and doing an exploratory surgery. They went in, and what should have been a seven- to eight-hour surgery turned into about an hour and a half. They closed me up, and they came out, and told my wife, "Sorry, there's nothing we can do. He's got pancreatic cancer. The largest tumor is right at the head of the pancreas. We cannot remove it because that's where all the blood vessels come together. The only thing we could do was sew him back up." From there, we started the treatments and started changing my life.

When the doctor told my wife, he said, "Do you want me to tell him or do you want to tell him?" She said, "I'll tell him." She came in the next morning, and said, "Okay. The bad news is you've got pancreatic cancer. They gave you six months to a year to live. The good news is you better hurry up and get out of here, because you've got trash to take out at home." So from Day One, even though it was hard to do, we found the good in it. We could either focus on the bad part of it or we could pick out the good things. I chose, as part of my own mental therapy, to focus on the good things. I would tell people, "I've got pancreatic cancer." They would look at me and say, "Oh, I feel so sorry for you." And I'd say, "Don't feel sorry for me. I may have cancer, but my cholesterol is one-eighty." How many people can say that? The first oncologist I had was a guy like me. He had a sense of humor. I went in for my chemo treatment one day and he walked through the treatment room and said, "How you doing?" I said, "Well, not too good. I got sick right before I got here. I ate lunch and then I got sick." "Well, what'd you eat?" I said, "Well, I had Mexican." He said, "Well, that tells you something." I said, "What does that tell me?" He said, "Don't eat Mexican." And he kept walking. We always kept a good attitude toward it. Attitude, to me, has always been a big part of it.

In March, I started a chemotherapy treatment, which consisted of two drugs called Gemzar and 5FU. I started radiation therapy almost at the same time. I had six weeks of radiation therapy five days a week. Those were basically the only two therapies I had. Before I started, we discussed the immediate side effects. On the chemo I was told that it would make me tired and give me nausea. They also told me that with my particular type of chemo and the location of my cancer, it was doubtful that I would lose my hair. But I did. I didn't lose all of my hair, but I lost it in patches. Just small patches here and there. The chemo also changed my hair color. Originally I was blond-haired. Then when it started falling out in patches, I shaved it all off. But when it grew back, it grew back brown. They said that was caused by the chemo, because it changes the chemical makeup of your cells. I was told that there wouldn't be that many side effects from the radiation therapy. The only side effect I might actually feel was like a sunburn. But back to the chemo: Out of a seven-day week, I might have two good days. And it was usually the day of the chemo treatment and the day after. The thing that was bad about it was that my doctor set me up to receive treatment on a Wednesday, which meant that by the time the weekend came around, I was out of it. So my weekends shifted to Wednesdays and Thursdays.

As far as long-term effects go, I probably have what some people know as chemobrain. I had never even thought about it until I had it. After you've been on chemo for a while, your thoughts get jumbled, you slur your words, and you start thinking, "I never did this before. Why am I doing it now?" And then you come to realize that it's chemobrain. Other than that, I've had no long-term effects from the chemo. In December of 2001, I went in to have the same thing as a gastric bypass. They had to go in and cut out a part of my stomach that was scar tissue from the radiation therapy. I was supposed to be in the hospital for just a week, but I was there until February 17, 2002. The first surgery didn't take. They had to do a second one in which they ended up taking out three-quarters of my stomach. I ended up with two staph infections, blood clots on my lungs, and infections in both my central ports. But I made it. To me, it was just another battle I had to fight.

Those surgeries left me with physical side effects as well. Before all this started, I weighted two hundred and ten pounds. I now weigh one thirty-eight on a good day, or on a fat day, like my wife says. I used to be a sweets lover. Now, sweets go right through me. As soon as I eat something sweet, five minutes later, I'll start cramping up. I've made some changes in the past five years. As far as eating differently goes, I now have to have five or six small meals a day. I can't eat like a normal person and have three meals a day. That in itself takes a lot of getting used to. I also have to watch my sweets intake. With three-quarters of my stomach gone, everything I eat is digested and almost through my system within three or four hours after I've eaten it. So it changes habits all the way around. I also get tired easily. I bruise easily. I cut myself very easily. There was the possibility that with 80 percent of my pancreas cut out, I would become a diabetic. But I was lucky. I'm not diabetic at all. All these physical side effects are not only from the surgeries but also long-term side effects of the chemo.

I'm fifty years old now. I was forty-five when I was diagnosed with pancreatic cancer. And a year before that, when I was forty-four, I was diagnosed with lung cancer. They took out half my lung, a mass from my left breast, and half of one rib. Which, by the way, grew back. I didn't know it, but ribs grow back. Whether the pancreatic cancer caused the lung cancer or not, we don't know. A lot of people have asked me if it has metastasized anywhere else in my body. That I can't say, because usually pancreatic will metastasize to the liver or the lungs or the stomach. As I was diagnosed almost a year prior with lung cancer, I can't say if the pancreatic caused the lung cancer or what. They say lung cancer cannot cause pancreatic, but pancreatic can cause lung. So I don't know, because at the same time, I was a smoker. It's still a toss-up.

I discovered the lung cancer differently than I did the pancreatic cancer. I had noticed a lump on my left breast and lived with it until even my shirt rubbing against my nipple made it hurt. So I went to the doctor, my primary physician, for that. They did an ultrasound to find out how thick it was. I'm one of a very few men who can sympathize with a woman when it comes to a mammogram, because that's what I had next. It wasn't a fun thing to go through. They also did a chest X-ray, which showed a dark mass on my left lung. So my primary physician suggested that I go see a lung specialist. The lung specialist did a bronchoscopy on me. He called me up and said, "I'm referring you to a surgeon. You've got lung cancer in your left lung. Your right lung is totally clear, but in your left lung, you have cancer." I went to the surgeon and asked him what we do next. He scheduled a mastectomy and a lumpectomy at the same time. They went ahead and got both the mass on my breast and the cancer in my lung at the same time. The mass on my breast turned out to be benign. They took out half of my left lung. I didn't have to have any chemo or radiation therapy after that. They took it all out. In October of '98, I went back to the surgeon for a CAT scan and a chest X-ray. They both showed that the surgery had been successful and gotten all of the lung cancer. I was happy with that.

But then, in November, I started having digestive problems: acid reflux and what felt like heartburn all the time. They did an ultrasound and said that I had gallstones and that I need gallbladder surgery. So I went in and had that done. But I still had digestive problems. We tried Prevacid and that didn't work. Rolaids and Tums didn't work, either. So they did another ultrasound. This time they said I had cysts on my pancreas. That's when they suggested doing the Whipple procedure and going in and removing them. That was February of '99. They went in and came back out, and that's when the real battle started. The first battle with lung cancer, I figured, "Okay, well, that's over and done. I'm glad it's out of the way. I won that war." But no, I didn't realize that that was just the first of many battles to come.

I wrote in a journal. When I first found out I had cancer, I started putting down different thoughts that I had about different things. "Today has been yet another day in my life: a life in which it took thirty-one years to find love; a life which has had good times and rough times." Definitely rough times, yeah. "You may read this and ask yourself, are these the thoughts of a dying man, or the rantings and ravings of a lunatic? Be not alone, for this I ask myself every day." I would just write down my thoughts on these things because it would make me feel better. Some of them were good thoughts, some of them were bad thoughts, but they had to be written down, because it was part of what I considered therapy for myself. You know, even five years later, recurrence is still in the back of my mind, even though I know that now that I've made that five-year anniversary mark, it's less likely that it will come back. I understand that, but still in the back of my mind it's there every day. Am I going to make it from here on out? If I don't, I'll fight the battle again. I don't care. I know how to do it again. I've done it. I'll do it again.

My wife took it very hard, but she's been the best caregiver I could ever have. It was both good and bad with the rest of my family. I've got a son who doesn't want anything to do with me. There are some other issues there, but in part I think he's scared that if we get too close I won't be around long enough. I've got a stepdaughter who I love to pieces. She's like my own daughter. If my wife couldn't have been my caretaker, she would have done it. She was right there with us through a lot of it. My mother knows I've got it, but she doesn't want to believe it. My friends have reacted differently. My best friend would call me up and say, "So, I know you're on chemo. I know you don't feel good, but I'm going fishing tomorrow, and you're going with me." But some other friends dropped by the wayside, because they were scared, I guess. I suppose it's understandable to a point. If one of my best friends walked up to me today and told me he was dying of the same thing I had, I don't think I would walk away from him, but then you can't explain somebody else's feelings toward it.

Attitude makes a big, big difference, even for the caregivers. You know, a lot of the caregivers I know will say, for example, "Well, her appetite has dropped," and they're discouraged. So I say, "Have you tried giving them some of these different liquid meals that are available?" They say, "Well, yeah. They like this one, but they don't like this one." I say, "Okay, fine. If they like vanilla, take the vanilla. What kind of fruit do they like?" They say, "Well, they like oranges." I say, "Fine. Make a smoothie. Put it in the blender. Live a little dangerously. Leave the top off the blender every now and then." Attitude! Find something good in it, you know. Aggravate the patient. Ask them all the time, "Are you hungry? Do you want something to eat? What do you want to eat?" Let them tell you what they want to eat. And if they say, "Quit aggravating me or I'll strangle you," say, "Ha! You don't have the strength to strangle me." Make them mad every now and then. There were times when I didn't want to get out of bed. My wife would come into the bedroom and say, "Well, honey, come on, get up. At least come and sit on the sofa. You know, if you'll sit up for five minutes, then you can lie down for an hour." We would compromise. Find something in between. It's almost harder for the caregivers than for the cancer patient. I really feel like sometimes it's a little tougher for them. But I can't stress it enough: There's always got to be a positive attitude. If you dwell on it, it's just like anything else that's bad: The more you dwell on it, the bigger and worse it'll seem. You have the power to make it as large or as small as you want to.

Attitude. I'm one of these people who always takes a positive attitude. If I take a positive attitude toward it, then it can't be as bad as if I didn't. I told my wife at one point, "I've come to the decision that since I have it, I have to decide how I'm going to control *it* and not let *it* control me." "It" being the pancreatic cancer. No way was it going to control my life. I still wanted to live. My surgeon at the time told us that if I had any life insurance, retirement money, 401k savings, cash, whatever, that we should cash it in and have a good time because I only had six months to a year to live. You know, "Enjoy it while you can." Well, we did that. But here it is now five years later. I'm broke, but I'm alive. That's attitude.

I can't work anymore. I feel at times that I could work, and sometimes I wish that I could work, but I don't. Social Security says I can work. They sent me one of those "go back to work" cards. You know, it's almost like a "get out of jail free" card in Monopoly. "Take this card in to any employer. They're guaranteed to hire you, and we guarantee it won't cut into your Medicare." But there are still days when I can barely get out of bed. I still have to push myself some days to get out of bed, because I hurt. The pain is not from the cancer now. It's from the after-effects of the cancer, the surgeries and the radiation therapy. But then there are other days I get up and nobody can keep up with me. It'd be nice if I could find a part-time job where I could call them up and say, "Hey, I feel good today. I'm coming in to work." But it doesn't work that way. So I find different things to fill my time. I do yard work here and there. I write. I build little projects, help people out doing little things here and there. Just things to keep busy. It's work, but not what most people would call work.

But the medical bills and not working have affected my everyday living. Before I had the cancer, my wife and I would take off and spend a weekend in Tunica visiting the casinos there. We lived in a nice furnished apartment right across the parking lot from a golf course, an Olympic-size swimming pool, and a clubhouse. After I had the cancer, my monthly income went down by about half. But even if I hadn't taken all of my retirement and done what the doctor told me, five years later it still would have been gone, because if I hadn't done it to have fun, I would have had to do it to pay the medical bills. It's just another battle you have to overcome. You have to adjust. It's hard, but you're thankful every day that you're still alive. Money is just money. It can't "buy" you permanent health. It can improve your health, but it can't ensure your health. Just like money can't buy you happiness.

Survivorship is being able to say I came close but I survived. I overcame it. The odds were against me, but I turned them around in my favor. That pretty much sums it up for me right there. If it wasn't for that word "survivorship," and me wanting to get to that point, then those odds would have taken over a long time ago, and I wouldn't be able to say today what survivorship means to me.

I'm David Driver. I am a six-year lung-cancer survivor and a five-year pancreatic cancer survivor.

Live strong.

"Have every teenage girl lose her hair for six months and she'll be a much better person."

AMY**DILBECK**

I became a cancer survivor on March 14, 1986, when I was diagnosed with osteosarcoma.

When I was diagnosed, I was fifteen years old, a month away from my sixteenth birthday. Osteosarcoma is basically a very rare and very aggressive form of bone cancer. It started in the center of my right femur and ate its way outward through the bone, so that by the time we found the tumor, it was about four inches in diameter and had made my bone hollow to the thickness of an eggshell. That was causing parts of my bone to break off and float around in my bloodstream, which was causing a lot of the pain that initially alerted me to the fact that something was wrong.

I was in high school and really active in swimming and cheerleading. I had just been elected junior-class president when I started to have pain. From that point on, it was a series of doctor's visits. On the third visit they said, "Well, maybe this is more than a pulled muscle. Maybe we need to take an X-ray." From the X-ray we could tell that there were some parts of my leg that were a little bit shaded. So the radiologist called and said, "You need to get her to the children's hospital as fast as you can." And at that moment my life changed very drastically.

My treatment began with lymph-salvage surgery. What they did was go in and replace all the bone that had been affected by the cancer with metal. There are a lot of different muscles moving around the bone going to different places in order to move the leg. When I had the surgery on my bone, many of the muscles were slightly displaced. What that means is that the muscles that were used to moving in one way were now a little bit different and had to move in a new way. So, for instance, I had to figure out how to run again. It became something that I had to think about. When I used to run, I would push off with my foot one way. But I found that I had to modify what was happening within my body because it didn't work the same way that it had. In order to relearn how to walk, run, and jump normally (or as normally as possible), I had to think about movement in terms of the small processes that come together to make one big movement.

My physical life changed a lot after I was diagnosed and all through treatment. I wasn't allowed to go to school for most of my treatment, so I was away from my friends. It was more than just not being able to walk correctly. During treatment, I didn't have the strength to physically walk down the hall to the bathroom by myself. I went from swimming competitively, cheerleading, and walking up and down the hall with my books at school, to not being able to do anything on my own. So there were things that I really longed for and really looked forward to doing again. There were times it the hospital that I was so sick that I couldn't go outside for very long. My mom would wheel me out in my wheelchair, and I'd just sit there in the sun for ten minutes and feel the wind on my face. I was remembering the things that I wanted to do. I was excited about life after cancer. That motivation really helped me to get through my treatment.

Still, not being able to move in most ways without having someone help me brought on a lot of emotional baggage. There's a lot of spiritual change that happens during that loss of control, and I think it does one of a few things to you. It either makes you want to fight a lot harder to get back to your old life, or it makes you give up. You have to make the choice between those two things. I chose to fight really hard and to assert my independence in other ways than by walking. Maybe I couldn't carry my own books to class, but I was going to get an "A" on that paper. Or maybe I couldn't swim right now, but as soon as I could swim I was going to win a race. Thinking about hope for the future, being excited about other things and realizing that there was change within my body, were what made me get better.

I had to go through a lot of physical therapy after my surgery. It started very basically with learning how to use my muscles again. After having been in bed for so long and having such an extreme surgery, my muscles literally didn't remember how to move my leg anymore. I had gotten pretty good, during chemotherapy and treatment, at modifying all my behavior so that I would use only one leg to walk on crutches or use a wheelchair, whatever I needed to do to move around. But when I really started to focus on walking again, I needed strong determination to remind myself that this was something that I wanted to do, had to do. I started off going to physical therapy about three times a week for two to three months. After that, my life was so busy that I didn't go back for appointments very much. I felt that once I had gotten to the place where I could move myself around a little bit better and where my muscles were starting to remember how to work, the best way for me to get better was to do things that I liked to do anyway. So I would take a walk around the block with my dog, and I would think about the way that my muscles were moving and how I wanted them to move and focus on walking a certain way. I would go to cheerleading practice in high school and focus on moving. I went back to swimming for my swim team. I did things that I loved to do before the surgery and things where I could focus again on using the muscles and on remembering how to move. Remembering what I was living for and wanting to do those things again became an important part of my physical recovery as well.

As a teenager diagnosed with cancer, one of the hard things to figure out emotionally is how you interact with the opposite sex. I was sixteen years old, balder than a cucumber, about one hundred pounds, and pale as a ghost. I felt like there was no way I could have been less attractive to someone. That was a hard part of being in high school for me, feeling like there wasn't anything about me that would be attractive or special to someone else. So dealing with finding your worth in who you are and not in what you look like is an issue that takes a lot of thought but ultimately makes you a better person. Have every teenage girl lose her hair for six months, and she'll be a much better person. I never wore a wig. I cheered at my high school football games without a wig while on crutches. Not wearing a wig and being bald in public was my way of saying that I was okay, that I didn't have anything to be ashamed of or need anything to hide behind. It was also a way to make people identify and understand what I was going through. It was strange for me during this time, when I had to deal with all these life issues like whether I was going to live or die, what these treatments were doing to my body, and how I was interacting with my family and my parents and with the world at large. I suppose it showed me the smallness of the regular teenage problems I was also caught up with. Relationships with the opposite sex, what you were going to wear to the prom, who had the newest shoes at school, and which physics teacher was the hardest; those things are pretty insignificant in the scheme of things, but can still be hard on you as a teenage cancer patient and survivor.

I reacted very strongly to my new scar at first. I actually couldn't look at it for two or three weeks after my surgery, mostly because it felt really foreign to me. I felt that it didn't represent who I was and that it wasn't part of my body yet. It took a while for me to get used to seeing it and accepting it. But after I decided that it was okay and I embraced it on my terms, it wasn't long before I started being pretty flamboyant about it in public, wearing skirts and shorts, and seeing it as

something that made me different and special, not different
and weird.

One of the biggest things that helped me to learn how to
deal with my new body and my new scar was sharing with
other people and being open about what was going on in my
life. Sharing made it easier for others to understand who I was
and also who I was in transition to becoming. My policy was
always to talk to anybody who wanted to hear about it and to
be as open as possible about what was going on in my life. I realized that in order to be accepted for who I was, people had to
understand who I was. And if I wasn't willing to share that with
people, then how could I expect them to know me?

I probably tell people, depending on the day and the circum-
stance, three, four, five, ten, twelve times a day about what
happened to my leg. People ask because they're curious. But
having those conversations so often can be really draining and
tiring. A good friend helped me realize that I didn't need to tell
everyone the whole story, "Amy, you know, you don't have to
tell everybody that you had cancer. You can just say, 'I had knee
surgery . . .' and that's enough, if you don't feel like talking
about it." Understanding that it was important to be open, but
also choosing when to be open, was really freeing for me. It was
okay if I didn't want to give all of my information to every person on the street. There are people who don't deserve to hear
it, people whose motivation is sheer curiosity. They don't care
about me as a person—they just want to know what happened.
They are looking at my leg, and they wonder, and they ask
without thinking at all about how I might feel about it. At the
same time, I think it's always important to respond to those
people with kindness and patience.

I've had people respond to me a lot of different ways about
my scar and my surgery. I've encountered kids who ask and
when I explain to them what happened, they look at me and
say, "That's gross." Some adults have actually said that, too. One
of the things cancer survivors learn is that some people simply
don't know what to say. Someone will ask you about your scar

or about your experiences, and when you give them the answer, they're just struck dumb and don't know what to say. Of course there isn't a standard response or one that is always appropriate. Interacting with others who are curious about my illness has given me a new way of understanding myself. How I respond to those people affects how they respond to me. Understanding how to interact with people on a different level when it comes to your health is something that takes some growing into.

Emotionally, a lot of things changed after my diagnosis and after my surgery. My friendships in high school changed, because a lot of people didn't understand how to deal with what was going on with me. Instead of dealing with it, they either tried to ignore the cancer or ignore me. And both of those can be pretty hurtful. At the same time, though, there were a lot of people who surprised me with how incredible and thoughtful and consistent they became in my life. It's something that I took as it came and that helped me to deal with the people who were not able to understand me, but it also prepared me for special surprises and blessings from people that I may not have expected them from.

Things also changed for my family in many ways. My mom and dad became really focused on me. I have a little brother and a little sister, and I know that my sickness was hard for them. In many ways, I was the center of attention at every family event, every social event; my sister said that for nearly a year nobody asked her about herself. They all said, "Hi, Kathy, how's your sister?" My little brother was little enough that he didn't understand a lot of what was going on, though now he says that he wished people had told him more. He says that he and my sister often worried about what was going on with me because people thought that they didn't understand and didn't need to know. Instead they imagined things that were probably much worse than what was actually going on.

There's a huge sense of connectedness between my parents

and me. They gave me so much during treatment and recovery. They were the ones dealing with things. You know, I'm sleeping for three days on chemo and drugs. But my mom's the one up talking to the nurses, making sure that things are okay, rubbing my feet, getting me bananas, doing all those things that I couldn't do for myself. I think that even after treatment the emotional connection between the survivor and the parent is very strong. My mom will probably always be more protective of me than she is of my brother or my sister. I get a sniffle and she thinks that I need to call the specialist because it might be something serious. I stay out past midnight and she's worried I've been in a car accident.

Even now, eighteen years later, when I go back for my checkups at the clinic, my mom is the one who can't sleep for a week before. But then as soon as we get out of there with an "Okay," and good scans, you can just see her kind of relax back into the seat. She never wants to tell me that she's nervous beforehand, because she doesn't want to make me nervous. But she is nervous, and then she always tells me on the way home that she was a wreck all week. One of the interesting things that has happened in my relationship with my parents has been the increase of pressure to do something special, like change the world, because I'm a cancer survivor. It's like I've been saved, so to speak, so my life must have some higher purpose or calling. That can be stressful. But, as I come farther and farther in my journey of survivorship, I've realized that it's okay just to be me. My parents also still say funny things to me like, "Honey, you are a cancer survivor and you are different. So if you get tired at work, you tell them that you need to take a nap." Or they'll say, "We don't want you working too hard. You don't need to put in any overtime, you need to be there from eight to five and that's it, because you are a cancer survivor. You don't need to work too hard." And I think, "Who else's parents in the world tell them that they don't need to work too hard?" It's kind of surreal. But I don't listen to them. That's the funny part. I work late all the time. They would love it if I just moved back home and stayed with them. If they could watch me and put some sort of plastic bubble around me so that I'd never stub my toe again, they would be super happy.

If I had one piece of advice I could give a caregiver, I would say, "Always massage the survivor whenever she asks." Seriously. That would be my first recommendation. But take care not to go overboard and baby the survivor. Don't give in to unreasonable demands, don't take care of them and think that they can't handle a lot of stuff on their own. It's an interesting and tough balance to strike, because there are times when the survivor *needs* help, but there are times when they don't *want* help. I think that the caregiver, the family member, the friend, or whoever, just needs to be aware of the fact that the survivor still knows what they want. It may not always be the best decision for them, but it's an important part of empowering that person and giving them back a little control over their life. I may want to move heavy boxes, and though it may not be the best idea for me to do it, I may just want to do it so that I can feel control over those boxes. I may want to get up on a chair in my bedroom and change the lightbulb by myself just because it's what *I* want to do. I may want to walk around the block by myself, even when it may not be the best choice for me. And I don't really know what the best recommendation is. Should you let them, should you not? Be aware of the fact that survivors still know what they want and that they still want to assert control and have a part in making decisions. That's really important.

When I finished treatment, there were a lot of different emotional and psychological things that started happening. For one, I was used to being the center of attention. I was used to being the person that everyone asked about, getting cards from all over the United States and being prayed for by friends and strangers. There was a sense that everything I did was the most important thing in the world to everyone around me. Once I got off treatment and was supposedly normal, returning to life as I knew it was shocking. I wasn't the center of attention anymore. I had to let go of a lot of things that had supported me for the last year of my treatment. It was hard to let go of chemo. It was hard to let go of the nurses and the routine, because my life, for whatever time period, was dependent on those things. Post-treatment is about how you redefine yourself as a person without the chemo, without the treatment, without the diagnoses. Who are you going to be now? How will you draw all those cancer experiences together and make yourself into the new person that you want to be? It's about being open with yourself and about learning from other people, taking your experiences and really letting them make you into a different and better person.

Not everything is serious all the time. One of my friends loves to make fun of me. She said, "When are you going to stop using the cancer crutch? We're all tired of hearing about your cancer story." And I said, "Well, you don't seem to mind when I pull out my handicap parking placard, now *do* you?" And she said, "Point taken, you win." One time we went to see a show in L.A. We got there late, and I had my handicap sign, so I thought, well we'll just park in the handicap zone and put up the sign. So we get out and the man who pulled up next to us only had one leg. So my friend looks over at me and says, "Limp," because you never want to be the jerk who parked in the handicap spot. I've also gotten yelled at more than once. I parked at the mall, and as we were getting out of the car, this older man pulled up in his car and yelled out the window, "You don't even have a handicap placard. Where is it? What are you doing parking in the handicap?" My sister looks at him and goes, "She has a handicap placard, and a two-and-a-half foot scar to go with it. Would you like to see?" He drove off quickly.

What was hardest for me about entering the job field and figuring out what I was going to do with the next three, five, ten years of my life, was trying to differentiate between who I was as a cancer survivor and who I was as just me. I also had to figure out whether or not I wanted to combine those two people. Did I want to pursue some career in a field that would incorporate those two parts of myself? Or did I want to be in a totally different place, where I never interact with people on the level of being a survivor? The more I thought about it, the more I realized that it would be really healthy and helpful for me to find some closure in the area of survivorship by working where I could help other people going through the same thing that I had. I felt that I could offer some insight into what was going on in their lives, as well as some guidance in what to look forward to and what to look out for. What I've learned along the way is that I have a lot of lessons to share with others.

To those people who are just starting off in cancer treatment, I would say, take it one step at a time. Start each day with the mission to be the best you can be and to do the best that you can. Do what you need to do. Listen to the doctors, get second opinions, but when you decide who you are going with, do what they tell you to do. Remember to keep some things in your life that make you happy and fulfilled and that give you other things to talk about besides how many times you threw up in a day or what kind of chemotherapy you're on.

To me, survivorship means learning about yourself through the process of treatment and chemotherapy and diagnosis, taking all that and putting it together with who you are as a person to make yourself even more incredible than you were before.

My name is Amy Dilbeck, I'm twenty-three years old, and I'm a bone-cancer survivor.

Live strong.

"Being on this side of the grass."

BRIAN**HILL**

I became a cancer survivor in 1997 when I was diagnosed with a squamous-cell carcinoma, which began on my right tonsil. By the time they discovered it, it had bilaterally metastasized to both sides of my neck and my lymph nodes.

All cancer treatments are difficult. Those of us who have been through them refer to them as the "slash," "burn," and "poison" technologies, because you either go through surgery or radiation or chemotherapy, all of which, no matter which one (or three), you get, are fairly devastating. Any surgery, especially a major surgery (I had the right side of my neck removed) is not only emotionally traumatic but physically traumatic as well. They had to sever a variety of nerves, muscles, and tendons in order to get to the structures they needed to reach. That nerve damage has consequences. Radiation treatments, while you're there receiving them, don't seem to be very much. But the radiation sickness that develops and goes on for months and months after the end of treatment is quite debilitating. And there's a loss of function from various things that happen long-term. I'm just now starting to have loss of function in parts of my face and in parts of my right shoulder as a result of nerve damage from the radiation. So it really doesn't matter which treatment you pick, there's going to be consequences that are difficult to deal with.

Another such consequence I've dealt with is xerostomia, which is the loss of salivary function. Acute xerostomia, which most head- and neck-cancer patients end up with after radiation treatment, is a result of the radiation beams destroying the salivary glands in the mouth. Depending upon where the tumor is, they may be able to salvage one or two, but most of the time the main ones, the submandibular glands, are lost in the process. I have only one little tiny salivary gland left behind my front teeth which produces a minuscule amount of saliva. Just the act of talking requires that I drink water constantly just to keep my tongue from sticking to the roof of my mouth as I'm making my words. It has also impacted my dietary habits. My cardiologist is very happy because I'm eating fruits and vegetables and other wet and healthy foods. All the things that I used to eat that are bad for me, like roast beef, I can't eat anymore. There are consequences that are less obvious than always needing a water bottle. Saliva has protective enzymes in it that keep you from getting tooth decay and periodontal disease. All those protections are gone. So, frequently, people who have had head and neck radiation are on fluoride trays all the time, every night, to keep the decay at bay. And instead of having their teeth cleaned once a year, they have them cleaned once a month. There are a lot of things like that involved. But there are many ways around them. For example, I ride a motorcycle and I've built a water bladder into my jacket, like Lance has on his fanny pack. I have a tube that comes around my shoulder so I can ride my motorcycle long distances without needing a water bottle to drink out of. I also fly an aerobatic airplane. It's one of my passions. Maneuvers that you normally have to have two hands to do on an airplane, like loops and rolls and spins, I can do with a bladder and a tube hanging over my shoulder. While the xerostomia is a consequence of radiation, it's a really small price to pay for being on this side of the grass.

The physical survivor issues that you deal with vary, depending upon when the disease is found. Patients diagnosed as early Stage I and Stage II may have a very minor surgery and may not have radiation, or they may have a new kind of a radiation called IMRT, which bypasses and targets around the salivary glands. Different people have different outcomes as a result of this. I haven't talked to any survivor who finds these difficulties, in the long run, major obstacles in life. Everybody is just so glad to have another chance that having a dry mouth doesn't really factor into life so much. Oral cancers are extremely survivable if they're caught early. If you're caught as a Stage I or II, you have an 80 or 90 percent chance of surviving and going on with the rest of your life. Unfortunately, early diagnosis doesn't happen often enough.

It's difficult to know if you're sick during the early stages of oral cancer. It can be very asymptomatic. You can have a little white spot or red spot in your mouth and not think much about it because it doesn't bleed or doesn't hurt. Part of the charter for the group I work with is to get professional awareness up and to make oral-cancer screenings as commonplace in America as having a breast exam or a pap smear every year is for a woman.

Seventy-five percent of the people who get oral cancers get them from some sort of tobacco use—spit tobacco or smoking tobacco, cigars, pipes, and so on. But I didn't smoke. Twenty-five percent of us who get this disease have no risk factors at all. Doctors believe that for those of us who didn't smoke, the cancer was probably caused by a virus, HPD, the same virus which causes 95 percent of all cervical cancer in women. It's sexually transmitted. Often, people who made bad lifestyle choices early on and smoked a pack a day for twenty years have feelings of guilt. You look at the average age of people with oral cancer, and ten years ago they were all over fifty and had smoking habits combined with heavy drinking. Now we're seeing a group of people in their thirties to their fifties who never smoked. They are the fastest-growing group of oral cancer survivors in the United States, and again, it's probably viral-related.

I'm no poster boy for living a clean life. But I think that you have to try not to beat yourself up about your past. We all do some things in life that are questionable. We make a lot of questionable choices. But once you have been diagnosed with something, your focus has to change. It has to change to dealing with the disease, getting through it, and moving on. If you live in the past and are constantly reliving—"God, I got this because I smoked or did this or that"—you're wasting positive energy that could be put toward getting well again.

I'm a very proactive person. I'm very aggressive and probably a control freak. So the worst part of being sick for me was the feeling of being out of control. I was in a situation where I couldn't do anything myself to effect change in my life. I could not make myself better. The best I could do was become my own advocate, and that began with finding the best care. But once I learned what there was to learn, I just had to put myself in somebody else's hands. I think the people at my hospital probably have characterized me as "the problem patient" because I had so many questions. I wanted to know why, I wanted to know what they were doing, I wanted to know why they were doing it, I wanted to know what the study said. They finally gave me the key to the hospital library just to get me off their backs, which actually only made matters worse, because I came in the next morning with more questions than I had the first day. I wanted to know about my disease. I found in talking to other cancer survivors that some of them only wanted to know so much. They didn't want to know everything, because it made them fear what was going to happen to them. But I don't think that's the right way to approach the disease. They always say that chance favors the prepared mind, so making the best decisions you can make when you're talking to your doctors is so important, because you do have options. You have options in treatment. The doctors can prescribe a particular treatment plan for you, though ultimately the decision is yours. I think that no matter how embarrassing a question it is, no matter how strange it seems, you need to ask it, you need to know, you need to understand, and you need to get it out there.

When I was originally diagnosed I was so overwhelmed by how often the words "cancer" and "death" occurred in the same sentence. I was really taken aback by it. I found that by having my wife with me at my meetings with my doctors, she heard things that I didn't hear. In the shock of it all, a lot of it just blows right by. They're telling you things—"You've got this, and we're going to do this, and it's this stage . . ." They're going on and on and I'm missing part of that and am confused, and she's up there scribbling notes. So when we got home, we were able to review everything that was said, what was discussed, and then go back with intelligent questions the next time around. So having somebody with you who is also paying attention and is not in the kind of shock you are helps a lot.

When you receive radiation, there's a period of time right afterward where you really can't speak. The larynx has scar tissue on it. Just saying, "Hi, hello," is a very difficult thing to do. But as time goes by, that scar tissue goes down a little bit. But my voice is very nasaly and very different from what it was. I'm missing some structures inside my mouth. My epiglottis, which closes off part of the back of your mouth when you make certain sounds, is pretty much gone. But look at me. I'm one of the lucky ones. I mean, there are people who lose their mandibles and have much worse happen to them. And even though it was caught very late, my cancer was still relatively localized to my neck and the inside of my mouth. It had not gone into my pharynx, or up into my nose or the orbit of my eye, or someplace else where these cancers do sometimes go. Issues of facial disfigurement, especially in our society where we are so oriented toward youthful people and people that look healthy and all that, are major issues for patients undergoing any kind of head and neck surgery. On the Web site that I help monitor, we have people who post their feelings about it all the time. I've seen them write, "I don't like to go to the store anymore and I don't go out to dinner as much. I wear turtleneck sweaters a lot," and some of them actually are reclusive and live behind the keyboard when interacting with others. I respond to them on the message board by telling them about this guy who jogs by my house. I've watched him for about a year now, and I only talked to him for the first time a couple of weeks ago. He's got one of these legs that's a big spring where his foot is. He's an amputee just below the knee. And I stare at him. I can't help it; he's different. But, you know, I marvel. He may see me staring at him and think, "God, he's looking at me because I'm weird or I'm different." But I'm not. I'm looking at him because he's such an inspiration.

There were a couple things I was not expecting from my facial radiation. About 3 to 5 percent of those who have facial and neck radiation develop nerve damage—not immediately after the radiation, but several years down the road. There are actually quite a few long-term effects from radiation. It's a cumulative effect during your lifetime. Around my third year out, when I really felt that I was as normal as a cancer survivor can feel, I developed the inability to control the corner of my mouth. I thought, "Wow, that's really strange. What's happening here?" At first I was thinking I had a little stroke or something, because my mouth and the side of my face started drooping a little bit. Then I started having what they call fasciculations where my trapezoid would just start going into violent contractions. My wife said on *Star Trek* there's a species of aliens called the Cardassians and they have these necks that look like lizards that kind of taper out with great big muscles, and my neck would just jump out like those creatures, like a whole inch. I had absolutely no control over it at all. When I went back to my doctors to ask about it, they said that about 3 to 5 percent of people get nerve damage as a result of the radiation. It won't get any better. It may get worse; but it won't get any better. That was something that I hadn't expected.

People lucky enough to be ten years out can still get an osteosarcoma related to radiation, because radiation itself is one of the things that can cause cancer. People who have received the

maximum doses of radiation can potentially develop other cancers. So here's this thing that saved your life and now it causes
a whole new thing down the road. I feel like I'm always waiting for the other shoe to drop. Your life is going along perfectly.
Everything good is happening. You've made money. You're
successful. You've got your sports car. You've got a long-term
relationship with somebody who makes you happy. And then
one day someone just pulls the rug out from underneath you.
That's an unusual experience for people, because usually you
have some kind of chance to see things coming. But this takes
you by surprise. After this has happened to you once, you're
kind of always waiting for what's next. When's it going to come
back, and what's going to happen? Now that the long-term effects of the treatment are known, some side effects can be pre-
dicted. You just hope that the cancer itself doesn't come back.

Every year, I go back for scans, MRIs and other tests, just to
make sure everything's clean. One of the tests is a spiral CT of
my lungs, to make sure that nothing has metastasized in that
likely region. I've been clean so far. But while my lung CT was
clean, the radiologist saw a little black spot on the top of my
liver. Inside I could feel my stomach come up in my throat. He
goes, "We really should look at this. It's only about five mil-
limeters across, but it's there." And I'm thinking, "Oh, not
again." I felt everything that I had felt the first time around all
over again. The rush of nerves and stomach acid and adrenaline
that went along with having him go, "What's this?" just
brought it all back. As a young guy I did time in Vietnam and
I was scared all the time, but I was able to choke it down and
get through each day. I find that now, as an older person, this is
harder for me to do. I'm becoming my grandmother, a woman
who worried about every little thing that was going to happen.
I can't go outside, because the dog next-door is going to bite
me and all these kinds of things. It's like the guy that I knew
thirty years ago in Vietnam has now become this little old lady
who is afraid of everything. It was then that I realized the impact that this disease has had on me. It's been a completely

personality-changing event. I think that's just part of survivor-ship. Almost every survivor I've talked to has had the same kind of experience, because nobody ever puts this completely behind them. It's a part of you from here on out.

I just wanted to live. I wasn't worried about coming out of sur-gery disfigured. That was the least of my worries. My first pri-ority was getting to the other side of the tunnel. I used to joke that the light at the end of the tunnel was an oncoming train and it wasn't really the new life that awaited me. But there really was a new life out there. And I'm completely different now than I was before. My life up until cancer was pretty much about me. I wanted to get ahead in business, I wanted to make money, I wanted to do the things that Brian wanted to do. Once I was given another chance, all of my priorities changed. So I wasn't worried about how I would be when I got through it, I just wanted to get through it and get on with this new op-portunity that I had.

I think that the cancer has made some good differences in my life. I had a chance to start a foundation for people with oral cancers. My fears, my anger, and everything else got channeled into doing something positive. Look at Lance. Not only has he competed in seven Tours, but there's this foundation and all these positive things are happening. There are people like that who take the negatives and turn them into positives. I'd like to count myself in that group. It doesn't mean that there isn't a lot of psychic debris that goes along with this. You cannot deal with people who are in the process of surviving without hav-ing some of it rub off on you every day. I've always wondered how psychiatrists deal with it, because the psychological debris that you pick up from dealing with people going through such tragedy is cumulative, and when you go home at night, some of that burden comes home with you. But then there are people on the message board who I talk to that come back and say, "I wouldn't have gotten through this day if you hadn't talked to me." And that just makes it all worthwhile.

Cancer emotionally changes people. My sensitivity and empathy toward others has grown. I'd been with my wife for seventeen years when I was diagnosed. She's an incredible lady and was with me through every step of this. The support that I got from her was just unbelievable. Our relationship is so much stronger than it ever was before. Talking about emotions is a difficult thing for guys. It's really hard to express and still be the stoic guy everybody expects you to be. It's different for guys in that we're used to internalizing things. We're the strong ones. We're the ones who deal with whatever has to be dealt with. But cancer can really take the wind out of your sails, and once that happens, a variety of insecurities can crop up. Sometimes the emotions start interfering with your ability to react to situations and to handle things that come up. We are so conditioned as men to just tough it out, suck it up and get through it. So when you feel emotional, it creates another thing inside of you saying, "Am I now less of a guy than I was before?" That really isn't the case, because I'm stronger now than I ever was. But it doesn't mean that the little insecurities and little voices aren't there sometimes.

When I came out of treatment, I was significantly depressed. It was beyond just being sad. Clinical depression sometimes requires medical intervention to help you through it. I went on some antidepressants to help me get through some of the thoughts that I had that were interfering with my emotional healing. As a guy, I felt vulnerable, and dealing with needing help was very difficult. In my parents' generation, the idea of going and seeing a psychiatrist was kind of verboten. You didn't do that. That was like admitting that you were unable to cope or unable to function in your daily life. But I found it to be one of the most satisfying and rewarding things that I've ever done. I learned so much about myself by talking to someone who understood what I was going through. I also felt that I did need medication to get through it. I don't think that I would have had as rapid a return to a normal perspective on life as I had without that professional assistance. I think if anybody, man or woman, has any insecurities about opening up to somebody, then they really need to seek out an objective professional to talk to.

I had an extremely successful professional life before cancer. I made a lot of money. I had high-powered jobs in big Fortune 500 companies. I was entrepreneurial. I started businesses that were sold for large sums of money. Two or three years after my cancer treatment, after not having worked for a little while, I went back to interview for some jobs at my level, CEO positions at international companies and such. I knew from working with the headhunter that I was more qualified than all the other candidates. I had two interviews and I wasn't chosen, and I thought, "How can this be? I've got the years of experience, I've got the track record, I've got the contacts in the industry to make this thing come together the way people want it to." After one of the interviews where I didn't get the job, I called the secretary back who had set up the interview, and I said, "Look, I realize that there's legal issues here that you can't discuss, but I just want to know if my discussing my recent cancer experience had anything to do with not getting the job, or perhaps there was a perception that I wouldn't be able to do the job properly, because I'm really 100 percent well." And she said, "Off the record, this was a factor. You mentioned in the interview that you were recently out of it. You mentioned there was the possibility that you could have a recurrence." So it was on their minds. They're planning on putting hundreds of people and millions of dollars of their money under my control, and it was on their minds. So a less-qualified person got the job. On one hand I was surprised by it, because I knew I could really go in and kick butt for these guys, really do a good job. But on the other hand, in their position I might have made a very similar decision. So after being turned down for a couple of jobs, I just decided I would create a job for myself. But I think that in the world of business, and I say this as a businessperson and not as a cancer survivor, that there are hard decisions you have to make, especially when you're dealing with stockholders and other people's money and other people's responsibility. You have to make the best decisions you can. Is that advocating prejudice? Is that advocating discrimination? I don't know. I've been on both sides of it now. I've made those kinds of decisions and I've been on the losing side of those decisions. I think the best advice is to always be honest. That's the best you can do. And hope that people will find that you're bringing something that has value that is beyond the risk they're going to take by taking you back in. So I started the foundation. I never worked this hard when I was getting paid to work. It's been a lot more fulfilling than anything I would have done for pay for somebody else.

Survivorship means having a second chance. I was sure that with Stage-IV cancer I wasn't going to be here for very long. But coming through it, I've realized how lucky I am. I spent most of my life wasting my time doing frivolous things, from chasing women to driving fast cars, doing all the things in life that are essentially unimportant. Cancer snaps you right back into reality, and you start making value judgments on how you want to spend your day. What can I do that is the *best* thing I can do today? How am I going to spend my time? What am I going to think about? I looked inside myself and found that I really didn't like myself that much before. But now I had this new chance. It's a shocking thing. We're not encouraged in this society to do that. Other societies are extremely geared toward a more spiritual sense. When I was in Vietnam, we spent some time next to a Buddhist temple. I had a chance to converse with a young Buddhist. He wore a small bone on a string around his neck. I couldn't resist asking, "What is that you're wearing around your neck?" And he said, "This is the finger bone of my master, who taught me everything that I know." And I said, "That sounds morbid." He said, "Oh, no, this is to remind me that life is finite. That every day is valuable, and that one day one of my students will wear one of my finger bones around his neck to remind him that he has to live today and that he can't expect that tomorrow's always going to be there." That struck me so. But at that point in time, thirty years ago, I came back from the war to the world of hamburgers and jobs and just lost track of that until having cancer snapped it right back into focus again. Life is finite. You don't waste your time. There's just so little of it.

My name is Brian Hill, I'm fifty-five years old, and I'm an oral-cancer survivor.

Live strong.

"I'm not the only one this has happened to."

EDEN**STOTSKY**

My name is Eden Stotsky, and I became a cancer survivor on November 12, 1997, when I was diagnosed with rectal cancer.

I'll go back to when I was misdiagnosed the first time at the age of eighteen. I was misdiagnosed from eighteen to twenty-six. I had been complaining of abdominal cramping and constipation, diarrhea, weight loss and weight gain. The doctors told me all sorts of different things: lactose intolerance, inflammatory bowel disease, irritable bowel syndrome, Crohn's, colitis. I mean, I got all different things. And they would give me remedies to deal with this: "Don't drink milk," or, "You pulled a muscle. Don't use this particular piece of exercise equipment." So I would listen to them, and for a little while, I would feel better. And then the symptoms would come back, and I'd go see the doctor again. So I would complain again, and they'd come up with some bogus excuse why I was feeling this way, and I would listen to them again. This basically went on for eight years. I lived on the fourth floor of an apartment building, and one day after working out at the gym, I hiked up the four flights of stairs, walked into my apartment, and collapsed on the floor, because I couldn't take another step. I was completely aware and awake and conscious, and totally fine except that I had absolutely no energy. I remember lying there looking up at the ceiling and saying, "Something is seriously wrong with me." So I went to my primary-care doctor, and that led to a whole barrage of appointments with gastroenterologists, colorectal surgeons, and oncologists. I was finally diagnosed by a colonoscopy on November 12 of 1997. I had surgery three weeks later to remove a tumor that was the size of an orange in my rectum. Can you imagine sitting on an orange? I don't know how I did it. I think about it a lot. My god, wasn't that uncomfortable? I think I just had a high threshold for pain. So I had the orange-sized tumor removed, and then I recovered for about four or five weeks. Then I had chemotherapy for six months and radiation therapy for six of those weeks in addition to the chemo. Everything happened really fast. I mean, I was diagnosed on November 12, '97, and I finished treatment June 5 of '98. I was done, finished, no more after that. Now I go for follow-ups. I get CAT scans, and PET scans, full blood-work and chest X-rays.

The surgery that I had was the "lowest" attachment that my surgeon had ever done. To be a little bit graphic here, frequently when a patient has rectal cancer, they end up with an ostomy, because they remove the entire rectum as well as the anal sphincter muscles. And if they have to remove the anal sphincter muscles, then there is nothing there to stop anything from coming through. So they automatically get an ostomy. I was very fortunate in that the surgeon was able to preserve the anal sphincter muscles. And because I'm a woman and the pelvis area is a little bit wider, they were able to pull down a little bit more of the colon to attach it. I was very, very, very fortunate.

Fecal incontinence was something that I was dealing with before I was diagnosed, and that I continued to deal with right after I was diagnosed, before I had surgery, and then after I had surgery while my bowels were trying to figure out how they were supposed to work with their new plumbing system, how they reconnected. So sometimes I would not make it to the bathroom. Sometimes I would barely make it to the bathroom.

And even now, if I have to go to the bathroom and have a bowel movement, there's not much time for me to wait. When I have to go, I have to go. It's not a fun thing, but it's something I've gotten used to. Anytime anyone needs to know where a bathroom is, they know they can ask me, because they're pretty certain that I've been to that bathroom wherever we might be. That's just a way of life. But it's certainly an embarrassing thing. It's not so much anymore, because I've gotten used to it, but there were times when I didn't make it to the bathroom and that was just something that I had to deal with. You just clean up, move on, and get on with your day. I am fortunate that it isn't something that I have to continue to deal with now. But I know that there are some colorectal-cancer survivors who do, and it's just something they've learned to live with. There are things that you can wear and medications you can take to prevent things like that from happening.

I've changed my diet, not because of how it affects my digestive system or my bowel movements, but because of the type of cancer I have. I eat a high-fiber, low-fat diet. Right after my surgery, I ate a lot of meat and potatoes. It was on a no-vegetables, no-fruits diet because those things would really have caused an uproar in my body. It wasn't something I wanted to deal with. So for like six months after my surgery, when I had a craving for fruits and vegetables, I ate baby food, believe it or not. It cured that craving, even though it didn't taste so great. But it allowed me not to have to run to the bathroom.

I have a lot of long-term side effects. I think most of it's probably from the chemotherapy. My sense of smell is off-balance, totally off. People will smell things that I don't smell at all. And then I'll smell something that nobody else will smell. So I'm at one end of the spectrum or the other, but I'm never on the same page as the person I'm with, whoever that might be. My sense of taste is off as well. When I cook food, often nobody but me can eat it, because it's so spicy. I put so much spice into it, just so I can actually taste it. But then whoever I'm cooking for practically has steam coming out of their ears! So my sense of taste is a little bit off, but that goes with the smell part, I think. I definitely have chemobrain. There have been a lot of articles published recently that have validated short- and long-term memory loss for people who have had chemotherapy. I find that I've got both. That is extremely frustrating for me, because there are some memories that no matter how someone tries to bring them back to me, I can not recall at all. I often wonder, "Was I really there?" And my friends and family say, "Yeah. Yeah, you were there." I don't know for sure if it's from the chemo, but I wasn't like this before I had chemotherapy, so I have to think it's from that. And of course I go to the bathroom more than normal. That is a side effect from the surgery and the radiation. But I've really gotten used to that. And I've gotten used to the taste and the smell thing. But the memory thing is still really frustrating. And I suppose I have a fear of the cancer recurring. The biggest fear comes from having received radiation therapy and whether the cancer will come back where I had the radiation. I certainly keep a close, close, close eye on my whole pelvic area to make sure that nothing is changing, that the cancer isn't recurring, or I'm not developing a new cancer in that area.

Up to this day, my white-blood-cell count is really low. Six years out, it's probably not from the chemo, but they haven't really figured it out. My counts just never went back up. So I have to be really careful if I cut myself. I have to at the very least put a Band-Aid on it. In my job, where I'm around sick people all the time, I have to make sure I wash my hands really well. I don't put my hands in my eyes or in my mouth or anywhere else the germs might get in. I think I've only been sick maybe once, if even that, since my chemo. But I'm always told when I get my blood drawn, "Be careful. Your white-blood count is down. It still hasn't gone back up, so your immune system is still compromised." I just take all the precautionary measures.

My wedding was scheduled for September 6, 1998. So three months after I finished treatment, I was supposed to get married. There were questions: Do we keep planning this wedding? Do we not? Do we cancel it? What do we do? And the doctor said, "No, keep planning the wedding. Keep planning the wedding." My fiancé and I had planned to move to Arizona right after we got married. And I remember saying, "I can't. I can't leave my doctors right now." I'd had this life-changing experience, and I didn't want to be on the other coast from them. My doctors had told me that once I hit my five-year cancer-free mark, I was in remission and pretty much out of the woods. So I was using that as a gauge. I would not leave them for five years.

I was very fortunate with my surgery in that a couple months before I was diagnosed with cancer, an OB/GYN oncologist came to my hospital. He practiced this rare surgery in which they actually relocate the ovaries to keep them out of the area of radiation. When it was determined that I had rectal cancer, they realized I was going to need radiation. Had my ovaries stayed in their original location, they would have died from the radiation after the first treatment. It was a little bit scary, because they weren't actually able to definitively diagnose my cancer until I was in the operating room. So I didn't even know 100 percent going into the surgery that it was cancer. We were pretty sure, but there had been no definitive biopsies. So they had the OB/GYN kind of on call. They removed the tumor, did a frozen section in the operating room, determined that it was cancer, called the OB/GYN surgeon, said, "Come on in. Move her ovaries out of the field of radiation so she can have kids in the future." And so I woke up with all these questions. "Well, what happened?" And they told me that I didn't have an ostomy bag and that they moved my ovaries. Now my ovaries are attached to my kidneys. I am still producing eggs and will hopefully be able to have children one day.

But unfortunately, I often hear of young-adult cancer patients whose doctors do not address fertility. Sometimes they say, "We don't have time. We have to treat the cancer aggressively. There's no time to address fertility." Well, that might be the case, but how long does it take to go to the sperm bank? Or, how long does it take to realize you can move the ovaries out of the field of radiation or freeze some embryos? I hear about cases like that often and realize that I was very fortunate. I won't be able to get pregnant the conventional way. It will be through in-vitro fertilization. Hopefully, one day I'll be able to see if it really works.

When I was going through treatment, I did not feel sexually attractive at all. I did not want to be sexually active. At the time, I didn't want my fiancé touching me, just because I felt disgusting. My oncologist had told me that for a certain amount of time after receiving chemotherapy, it was not a good idea to be sexually active because any sort of bodily fluids that came out of me had some traces of that chemotherapy, which is toxic. So the doctor told me that, which made me feel kind of poisonous. You know, I don't want to be sexually active. Plus I was nauseated and just not myself. I didn't feel all that attractive having been stuck with a needle every day. And I had my scar, which was healing beautifully, but it just didn't help me to feel so sexually attractive to him, or to myself for that matter. Now, I'm comfortable with my scar and I don't have those side effects. So I'm much more comfortable and don't really experience too many issues like these as a result of my cancer.

I did end up getting divorced. I think it was somewhat related to me having cancer. My ex-husband had traveled a lot during my treatment, so he didn't experience the cancer journey the way I had experienced it. It's one thing to be a spouse of a cancer patient, to experience it secondhand on a day-to-day basis, but he didn't do that because he was very rarely around. So I think it was hard for him to understand how I continued on with my life and why I chose to do what I did after I was finished with the treatment. He didn't really understand any of it, and it was a life-changing experience for me. I had been a positive person before, but I became even more positive living each day to its fullest. I didn't sweat the small stuff. But I probably took that to the extreme sometimes, and I think it was sometimes hard for him to understand where I was coming from.

Conversations about children are always interesting, because I can't get pregnant the normal way. Sometimes my partner's like, "Well, what do you mean you can't? How do you know for sure?" And I say, "Trust me. I'd be on the cover of the *Journal of Medical Science*, or the Journal of Whatever, if I ever got pregnant the conventional way. It just won't happen. My organs aren't attached the way they originally were." Trying to explain that is always an interesting conversation. But the positive thing is that there are plenty of women out there who don't know if they can get pregnant. I see it with cancer-free friends of mine. They go through so many things from A to Z trying to figure out why they can't get pregnant and what they can do. I don't have to figure out what's wrong. I don't have to figure out what I need to do, whether it's artificial insemination or something else; I know what I need to do. It's just a matter of doing it. With me, there's no mystery. So I try to put a positive spin on it a little bit.

I'm in a support group for young adults with cancer now, and the topics of dating and when to tell your partner you're a survivor always come up. I always tell them immediately. My life is very centered around cancer-related activities. And if for some reason they feel that they can't handle that or that's something that's going to bother them, then I need to know that upfront. I'm proud to be a cancer survivor. I'm comfortable talking about it. I don't mind discussing colorectal cancer, or the issues that I dealt with as a young adult, or any other kind of cancer issue with anyone who comes my way. I'm usually upfront and honest right from the get-go. Sometimes that's a turnoff. Sometimes that's too much for the opposite sex to handle. I've got some friends who are young-adult cancer survivors who are also dating, who wait until the sixth, seventh, eighth date, because their cancer is just not that big a part of their life. That wouldn't work for me. If I were to try to wait for date number two or three, they would figure it out before then: "Oh, what are you doing tonight?" "Well, I have this meeting." Or, "What are you doing this weekend?" "I'm doing this." "Why do you do so much with cancer?" Why would I try to hide it? But other people's lives don't revolve around cancer-related activities so much.

Being so involved with cancer organizations and working for a cancer organization helps me to deal with my own experience with cancer. Being diagnosed at such a young age and not knowing whether I was going to live or die or what my life was going to look like after my treatment was over was very traumatic. I was fortunate when I was diagnosed because the Ulman Cancer Fund for Young Adults started their very first support group a few months later. But aside from that group, there was nothing else for young adults when I was diagnosed. So for those first five months, I was finding only older people or kids who were diagnosed. Now I want to be out there for young adults, helping the population that I was once a part of.

As far as health insurance goes, I was fortunate to have a really good plan. And working and being a patient at my hospital helped as well. The biggest problem I had was with the billing system. It was absolutely atrocious. Every time I got an Explanation of Benefits from my health insurance company, I would match it up to the bill before I would ever pay it. Sometimes I would get a second bill from the hospital, and I'd call and say, "Sorry. I have no proof from my insurance company that I owe you this money, so I am not paying this bill." Half the time they'd be like, "Oh, well, we didn't submit it to your insurance company." And I'd ask, "Well, why don't you try doing that? Then maybe I'll pay what I owe." My biggest piece of advice, and I tell my patients this now, is, don't ever pay a bill unless your insurance company has told you that you should pay that bill. And look at all of your Explanations of Benefits from the insurance company. I did have some problems with my mammographies. My mother had breast cancer. And follow-up studies for my type of cancer have shown that there has been some known genetic link between breast cancer and colon cancer, so I get mammographies. But because I was in my late twenties, early thirties, the insurance company rejected those claims. I had to get a letter from my doctor saying that the test was medically necessary. So I found that with most things that the insurance company initially rejects, as long as you get your doctor to write a letter saying that it's medically necessary, the insurance company will cover it.

It's important to work on changing the screening guidelines for colorectal cancer. They say that you should start at the age of fifty, but I was twenty-six when I was diagnosed. I was twenty-six when I was diagnosed as a colorectal-cancer survivor. I'm not the only one this has happened to. I hear about young adults being diagnosed with colorectal cancer all the time. Perhaps because of my job, where we see the rarest of the rare cases, I see young-adult colorectal patients all the time. So I would like to see the screening age changed. What most people, including the insurance companies, don't realize is that the most common symptom of colon cancer is no symptom. So by the time a person is diagnosed with colon cancer, it is already advanced. With all the new drugs, the treatment for colorectal cancer is astronomically expensive. So the insurance companies are being ridiculous. There's no reason why they shouldn't screen at an earlier age. They'd be saving themselves so much money.

I give talks four times a month about life after cancer treatment. And what I tell people, because I believe this myself, is that cancer is two illnesses. It's a physical illness, and it's an emotional illness, and the two have to be dealt with in different ways. You don't treat a physical illness the way you treat a mental illness. Cancer has definitely affected me emotionally. I have a more positive outlook than I had before. I'm sensitive to the fact that I'm a cancer survivor, and proud to be a cancer survivor. I don't wear my feelings on my sleeve as much as I used to. I let things roll off my back. It takes a lot, lot, lot, lot, lot to really make me angry or to annoy or frustrate me. On the other hand, it takes very little to make me happy. It has made me look at life differently. I've realized that life is too short to spend it being unhappy. There are certain things that are in my control and certain things that are not. I try not to spend too much time focusing on the things that are out of my control. And I spend more time focusing on the things that are in my control.

I think survivorship means living life to the fullest and being there for other people who have just been diagnosed with cancer. It's about showing them that there is life, not only during cancer treatment, but after cancer treatment, and that life can be just as full and rewarding despite being diagnosed with cancer.

My name is Eden, I am thirty-two years old, and I'm a rectal-cancer survivor.

Live strong.

"It turns you into a fighter."

STACY**HOLBOROW**

I became a cancer survivor when I was diagnosed with papillary carcinoma in January of 2000.

I didn't know I had cancer immediately. I went in for a general OB/GYN appointment and the doctor was feeling my neck, which is pretty standard, and found a lump in the back of my neck. She pointed it out to me and said, "Have you noticed this? Has it been here for a while? You know, you should just keep an eye on it." I'm a very freckly person, so I just kind of dismissed it as just another growth. After about a year, it started to get bigger. So I went to an ear, nose, and throat specialist, where they did a biopsy on it. And it came back showing that there were thyroid cells in it, which they thought was very odd, because the thyroid is more in the front of the neck and this lump was in the back of my neck. They said, "Well, you know, it's something that we should just keep an eye on." Another year went by and it was getting even bigger. And I decided, when I couldn't even wear a ponytail without this bump sticking out on the back of my neck, that I was just going to go in and have them take it off, which they did. It was still a very curious tumor because it was mostly thyroid cells. They thought they should go ahead and give me a CAT scan to see if there was anything else in there that they needed to be aware of. When my CAT scan came back, they noticed a very large tumor behind my esophagus. They felt it was important to go in there and get it out. At that point, I still really didn't think it was anything too scary. It wasn't until after the surgery that they told me I had cancer. They got most of it with the surgery and would continue getting rid of the remaining cancer with radiation treatments. At that point, it didn't really hit me. I thought, "Oh, okay, so I've got cancer. Hmm. Let's just roll through the motions here and see what happens next." Here I am four years later, but I still have it.

I had several radiation treatments post-surgery. I went in right away and had a very large dose of radiation. I had that treatment and then had to wait months before they could retest me to see where my cancer levels were. They had to wait a few months until most of the radiation eliminated itself from my body in order to get a good read. The tests showed that I wasn't cancer-free, so they decided to go in again and, four or five months later, have some down time, see where I was at again, and then determine how much more radiation they wanted to give me for the second round. The following year, I went through yet another radiation treatment, and that didn't do the trick. We decided to skip a year to see what would happen, but then my cancer levels doubled. So I was treated again this past October with more radiation. And then again, they discovered that it still hadn't gone down to zero, so I haven't heard the word "remission" yet.

They are treating my cancer as a chronic disease at this point. We're going to keep hacking away at it until it goes away. And that has been disappointing, because I was expecting the parade of, "Yay! It's gone. Okay, it's over. I can continue on with my life." But no. That hasn't happened. So what I'm experiencing now is more of a chronic illness, where I have to be constantly monitored and looked at and scanned and tested. In a way, I feel very protected because I'm watched so diligently. But on the other hand, I feel like there's a monkey on my back that I just can't shake, and it's very, very frustrating. I don't want to go through treatment again. It's not fun at all. I just want it to be over. So I'm trying to learn how to deal and cope with it. It's more of a mental issue than a physical one. I look normal to many people, but when they discover that I have cancer, they're like, "Oh, really? You do? But you're so happy and you're working and you're functioning like a normal human being. You're a mom and a great wife." But inside, you know, I don't feel that way all the time.

My kids are eight and ten. Thankfully the worst part—the surgery and everything—took place when they were four and six. It was easier for them to sort of just fluff everything off as kids do. They're so resilient. Mommy was just sick. Mom wasn't feeling good. She was resting in bed all the time. She had an ouchie. They were aware of things on that level. But as the years went on, they really started to question, "Why are you going away again?" Or, "How come we can't see you?" And it was very difficult for me to tell them that even though there was something really wrong inside of me that wasn't just a cold or the flu, I was going to be okay. It was hard for me to determine exactly how to tell them that I'm going to be okay even though there's something very wrong with me and that I may not be cured overnight, or that the medicine might not take it away completely. That was difficult for them to comprehend. When my oldest daughter found out that I had cancer, she was just beginning to learn in school about the use of tobacco and alcohol and drugs and things like that, and how these substances can cause cancer in people. She'd see commercials about lung cancer or breast cancer and how devastating it is. She would relate this cancer information to me and what I was going through until she finally asked me, "Mommy, are you going to die? Can I catch cancer?" That was very difficult. It's hard to explain to a child that there are so many different levels of cancer. And to a child, that can be very scary, because they may only relate cancer to death. It was hard to shelter them, but I did my best.

My husband tried to be very strong for me and for my

children. I felt guilty a lot of times, because there was so much I had to give up as a mother, and it was hard to relinquish that control to him. A lot of times post-treatment, when I was starting to function again as a wife and mother, driving the kids to school or to lessons, I felt things relax into normalcy again. But really inside I was hurting, or I was frustrated, or I wasn't feeling really well, and so I'd snap a lot. I'd be angry, and it would catch him off-guard, and there were arguments. There was a lot of, you know, "We need to clear the air here. I'm not feeling good." And, "Well, I'm sorry. I didn't mean to hurt your feelings." So I felt guilty a lot. I actually wished that there was someone who could completely understand where I was coming from. But it's impossible for anybody who's not going through it to truly understand. As close as I am to people—my husband, my mother, my children, my friends—nobody really, really understands. They try, but there's so much going on inside my head that they don't understand. I just feel frustrated a lot. But then at the same time, there is a closeness. Through all of the darkness and the hard times, I seem to have come out of it really with such a rock-solid foundation in my marriage. And I think, "Oh, thank God I've got this guy by my side. I couldn't go through this alone." Or, "Thank God I have this friend who is a constant shoulder for me to cry on and this ear I can just blab away into." So I've learned how to evaluate where I am with a lot of people, including my husband.

My side effects are normally related to a combination of not being able to take my thyroid-replacement medicine and getting radiation treatments. For my treatments, I'm hospitalized and given a very large radioactive iodine pill. Then I'm in quarantine for several days at the hospital until the radiation levels get down to normal, to the point where I can't contaminate anybody else. Even then, when I'm released from the hospital they recommend that I shouldn't be near my children and that I shouldn't sleep side-by-side with my husband during a whole

night. It takes time and distance. So I'll go away for four or five
days after I leave the hospital to sort of cleanse myself and drink
lots of fluids. But because they took my thyroid out when I had
the initial surgery, I take regulating medication that makes me
feel normal and supplements my thyroid, which my body needs
to function. When they take away my medication, which they
need to do before radiation, I feel a lot of side effects. I'm depressed. I'm tired. I gain weight. And so I come down off this
normal period of life, when I'm on my thyroid medication for
six to eight weeks, so that I'm at my lowest point, where my
body is more vulnerable but more receptive to the radiation. I
get real puffy in the face. My eyes swell. My skin is very dry.
My hair falls out. My brain is fuzzy and I feel sort of stupid. I'll
be mid-sentence and forget what I'm saying. My short-term
memory is gone. I feel sort of dizzy, you know, for eight weeks.
And then I'm treated, and that's a course of about a week or
two, when they don't give me my pill right away, the Synthroid
that they put me on to bring me back up again to where I feel
normal. And even then, when I start taking the medication
again, it takes a while for my body to absorb it and really kick
in. So there's yet another period of four to eight weeks of feeling sluggish and down. It could be sixteen whole weeks of just
feeling cruddy and not normal before I'm back to myself.

I've had some intimacy issues that are definitely related to the
hypothyroidism. At the lowest points, you just don't want to be
touched. I really withdrew, and it was hard for me to be open-
armed again. Everything took effort. It took effort to be happy.
It took effort just to function as a normal person. So that affected many aspects of my life, including intimacy with my husband. And, you know, I think as anyone would, he felt rejected
and like maybe he had done something wrong. But it had
nothing to do with him. It had everything to do with me and
the fact that I just wasn't in the mood. I had way too many
other things on my mind. There have been a lot of ups and

downs. Right now, though, things are looking really good. I'm at a point in my treatment where they don't think they're going to give me any more radiation. I've had so much that we're really afraid of my getting a secondary cancer from the radiation treatment itself. So I want to save any radiation that I can receive until later on in my life, when I really have to have it.

I did have side effects after the surgery, because my vocal-cord nerve was wrapped around this mass that they took out. Immediately post-surgery, I couldn't speak. I was whispering. And my doctors told me that it's a very common side effect when they have to manipulate the vocal-cord nerve to unwrap a tumor. They had to cut into the nerve. I couldn't talk for about eight weeks post-operative. That was extremely frustrating, because, again, I had children and I felt like I was always whispering. My kids would ask, "Why are you whispering all the time?" There was also the fear that I would never get my voice back. My doctors told me that it could take a year for that nerve to regenerate, and that if it didn't in a year's time that I would have to go in for another surgery so that they could operate on my vocal cords. Miraculously, eight weeks later, I got my voice back. That was something they didn't expect. They had said, "If you do get your voice back, it probably won't be the same. You might speak a little rougher. Your vocal cords could be permanently damaged." So I went through eight weeks thinking, "Am I ever going to talk again?" It was devastating to think that I would have to lose my voice or a part of my voice forever because of this operation. So it was seriously a miracle when I started talking again. I called my doctor and said, "Hi, Doctor. This is Stacy Holborow." And he said, "Who?" I said, "Stacy Holborow." And he goes, "Oh, my gosh! I can't believe it! You're talking again." I mean, he was just as surprised. He said, "I saw that nerve in there. It was tattered. You know, I—I've no medical explanation for this." I'm very thankful.

————

Just knowing that I'm not cancer-free is very scary. I go through periods of total frustration. Like, "My gosh. I can't do anything to make this go away." I think I'm doing everything right. I changed my diet. I'm exercising. I'm doing all the right things, but there's still remnants of this cancer inside me. It's like a silent invader. I can't feel it, but I know it's there. The doctors can see it in my blood. So it's a feeling that I have something in me that I can't control. Relinquishing that control and really depending on my faith and my hope that everything will be okay tomorrow is the only thing I can do. Everything will be fine, you know? But will it? There's always that question. Is it going to be okay tomorrow? Most days, yeah, it'll be okay tomorrow. But it's a struggle. There's the doubter in me and then there's the optimist in me. I struggle with that a lot.

I never thought I would have to treat anything chronic in my life. It's very frustrating because, again, you feel like you may look normal and at times you may feel normal, but when that doctor's appointment comes, when you have to go get your blood tested again or go through another body scan, it all comes back. So all that preparation that you've done, all of that which you've overcome to get your life back on track, gets derailed for a bit. All those constant trips to the doctor's office get frustrating. It's not easy to handle. But when you leave the doctor's office and you find out what's going on: "Yes, you still have cell levels left in your blood. We'll have to see you in six months," you still think, "Yay! I've got six months of freedom. Okay, here we go, back on the happy trail." Then again, six months later the doctor's appointment comes around and, "Oh, god, I have to worry about this again? I don't want to!" That's just something that I have to deal with in order to constantly try to feel normal. I put it in perspective, "Oh, it's no big deal. Things could be worse. It'll be okay." And usually it is okay.

I have had many fits of screaming into my pillow. I have felt angry so many times. It's not so much "Why me?" anger, or the "Why did this happen to me? Oh, my gosh. Woe is me," anger.

I've never felt that. I know it sounds funny, but I feel that I was given this experience for a certain reason. There's something in this experience that I am meant to learn, and I have. But I'm human, and this still sometimes just makes me so mad. Sometimes I'm just short of acting like a spoiled child, I just want to, like, throw things and scream about this disease. Why did it happen? Just why—why—why is it *in* me? And I feel angry that I can't stop it. I feel angry that as medically advanced as we are today, we can't get rid of it. I feel angry that even though I have never been diagnosed with a terminal illness, there are other people who have. I feel angry about the disease itself, not just papillary carcinoma but all the other cancers out there that people are getting. It's a very frustrating situation to be in. One thing that this anger has done, though, is made me a very tough person. Through my anger, I have learned so much about myself and I've learned so much about what to be thankful for in my life. So anger, to me, has been very frustrating to deal with, but at the same time, through the anger, I have gained so much insight about who I am as a human being and what is most important in my life, what kind of people I want to surround myself with. It's really shown me a lot of good things. Anger can be frustrating and hateful, but it's an emotion that, once you work through it, once you get past it, can allow you to see things in a different light. That anger is such an important part of the cancer process. Initially, it's scary and frightening. But it puts you into fight mode. You think, "Okay, I've got this disease. How am I going to make it better? What do we need to do here?" And that frustration and that anger drive you to do whatever you have to do to get better. It turns you into a fighter. So in a funny way, I'm thankful for being angry.

Survivorship means being able to deal with the cancer, being able to survive with the cancer. I wouldn't call cancer my friend, but it's in me. It's a part of me. And I am continuing to live my life and survive with this cancer inside my body. So survivorship to me is just living my life the best that I can possibly live it for myself, for my children, for my husband, and just trying to be happy and cohabitating with this disease.

My name is Stacy Holborow, I'm forty years old, and I'm a papillary-carcinoma survivor.

I live strong.

"We're going to cure you.
What more do you want?"

SUSAN**LEIGH**

I've been diagnosed with three different kinds of cancer. The first one started thirty-one years ago in 1972 when I was diagnosed with Hodgkin's disease at the age of twenty-four. That led me into oncology nursing. I decided that I wanted to really focus my career in the new arena of oncology, which they had just kind of coined the term for. It was brand-new. And one of the things that I had seen over the years was that nobody was really paying attention to what was happening to us cancer patients as we got further and further away from our diagnoses because they were so focused on this idea of cure. So I began looking into long-term late effects.

They've learned a lot from those of us who were treated back in the late '60s and early '70s, when cancer treatments had just been developed. At that time, they had no idea what it was going to do in the long run. But what they have learned from us since is that the therapy that we had been given should have been given in lower doses. They've improved on it since. So the physicians now tell me, "Gosh, Susie, if we had radiated you today, we would have given you so much less. It would be much more of a concentrated target than the huge area that they targeted back in 1972."

I was quite worried about the effects, and, after having done some work in late effects, I was diagnosed with breast cancer in

December of 1990. Eighteen years after the original treatment, hearing that I had cancer again was such a shock. I had been an oncology nurse and cancer advocate for so many years. I knew a lot about what the possibilities were. I also know that we don't know much about what happens to those of us who have developed second malignancies. We don't have much of a track record to look at. So I've never felt panic like I felt with that diagnosis. I'd felt the lump myself. I'd had a mammogram the year before and nothing showed up. But somehow I dealt with the panic, got through it, and then, because of my history, acted right away. I was on the phone to my gynecologist's office immediately. "Oh, we can probably see you in three weeks," they said. And I said, "Oh, no. Today. Somebody has got to see me today." Even if my physician couldn't see me, I needed to see somebody else. So they squeezed me in. I went in to see her late in the afternoon. After she looked at me, she said, "Day after tomorrow I want you in the breast clinic." Those two days were terribly nerve-wracking.

I went to the clinic and had an ultrasound. They said they were 99.9-percent sure it was a cyst and that I shouldn't worry about it. So I took the scans in to the breast surgeon, and he says, "Oh, looks like we've got a cyst to aspirate here." I went in, and he put the needle in and nothing came out. He put the needle in again, nothing came out, and after the third try he says, "I think we've got to take this out." So they took it out. For whatever reason, they always seem to do biopsies on Fridays and make you wait for the results over the weekend. "Oh, and don't worry about it over the weekend." Yeah, right. So I ended up coming back on the following Tuesday and finding out that it was in fact breast cancer. And it was a very frightening time for me, because I really didn't know what my options were.

But at least I had a team of people to work with. My job at the cancer center was sort of a safety net. I worked with so many people who were able to get in touch with the physicians who originally treated me for the Hodgkin's. Before I knew it, doctors around the country were deciding what to do with my particular situation. So I had a lot of good help, good guidance, and a lot of support getting through that.

That diagnosis brought up a whole different set of issues, because I had already had a lot of treatment for the Hodgkin's. I couldn't have the automatic lumpectomy radiation therapy because I had had treatment before. So I ended up having to have a mastectomy. I elected to have bilateral mastectomies. With that surgery completed, I thought that it was all over again until on my way back from an advocacy meeting in Washington, D.C., I was in a taxicab accident and fractured my pelvis. About six months later, the bladder problems that had resulted from the accident were continuing to increase, so they finally took a look inside. They accidentally found carcinoma-cytes to the bladder when they were looking at the other damage. It was kind of a coup that they found that so early.

One of the things I ask the physicians now is how much of this secondary and tertiary cancer is actually related to the original therapy that I had. Certainly we now know that breast cancer is now an increased risk factor for those of us who were treated as Hodgkin's survivors with such a huge amount of radiation to the chest area when we were younger. But they don't know about the bladder cancer. They can speculate that, because I did have some radiation to the abdominal area, it may have scattered and set up a process of carcinogenesis that actually happened about twenty years after the initial treatment. They are pretty confident in speculating that the radiation is one of the major risk factors. A number of medical articles about this have come out over the last ten years. I was diagnosed in 1990, and they started coming out in 1991 and 1992 when they really started looking at this population of long-term survivors and what risk factors they may have to deal with.

Chemotherapies have also been improved so they decrease the risk of late effects. So just because I've had these side effects surface doesn't mean that everyone who's been treated now or within the last decade will develop them.

What it does teach us is that we have to be acutely aware of our health follow-up and what that looks like in the future. Lots of people have said, "Well, gosh, if you'd known that you were going to develop breast cancer from the original treatment, would you have taken your original treatment?" And I say, "Of course I would have." It was the best they had to offer me at the time, and I wouldn't be around now to develop the other cancers or other late effects if I had not taken that original treatment. So my challenge to the medical community is that they start systematically following us and collecting information as to what is happening in our bodies, what kind of risk factors we have. Once the risk factors are known, then plans can be developed to either decrease those factors or detect problems earlier. The earlier we detect, the better chance we have of getting through that second crisis.

One issue that female survivors of previous cancers have is that our treatment options are going to be very different from those of someone who is diagnosed for the first time. Most likely, we'll be having mastectomies. And then there's the decision whether to have reconstruction or not. I did elect to have reconstruction, though I had tremendous difficulty healing due to all the damage to my skin from the radiation years ago. I actually asked the surgeons if I was going to have any difficulty healing as a result of that radiation so long ago. They looked at the skin and said, "Oh no, there's not going to be any trouble. It looks just fine." And then my general surgeon said, "Ummm . . . I took that first step, put the knife in with the first slice, and everything started turning blue." He said I probably had about half the normal vascularization and that it was damage directly due to the radiation. Nowadays they don't irradiate nearly as much tissue. It was much more difficult for me to heal than they originally anticipated. So it was a slightly different medical situation than other people who have not had cancer before would experience. But I got through it.

———

During my treatment in the early '70s, I dealt with some major physical issues. At that time, they didn't have any good anti-nausea drugs, so the nausea was incredible; the vomiting was incredible. It was this continual wave that went on, fortunately, for only about twenty-four hours at a time. Some people would have the nausea for two, three, or four days. Another thing that I remember vividly is that whenever they gave me the chemo, they also injected me with nitrogen mustard. Nowadays, people get Adriamycin instead. The nitrogen mustard would immediately give me this awful taste in my mouth. It tasted just like 409 cleaner smelled to me. So to this day, I can't stand 409 cleaner because it reminds me of that nitrogen mustard going in and the nausea that followed.

We've learned so much about the safe delivery of chemotherapies now that we can give people adequate anti-nausea drugs. When I received chemotherapy, and for years after that when I was an oncology nurse, we would have stacks and stacks of emesis basins. We knew people were going to throw up, so they were right there waiting for them. Nowadays, people are eating hamburgers while they are getting their chemotherapy. It's changed dramatically. Also, thirty years ago we didn't have what they now call growth factors, the special drugs that keep white- and red-blood-cell counts level. So our cells, our platelets, red cells, white cells, would continually go down as therapy went on, and there were times that we had to put off our therapy because those blood levels weren't up enough to let us safely take the next course. Nowadays, they can keep those blood cells at healthy levels, so that treatment can be received on a regular schedule. And that really improves the chances of getting rid of the cancer in a timely manner. It's really crucial to stick to those time frames.

We also didn't know how to deliver drugs quite as safely as we do now. We just kind of put it in any vein. And if you weren't in a treatment center at one of the very, very specialized cancer centers, the docs had no clue what to do. So they just gave you chemotherapy like they would give you anything in an IV, and it was really scary. As an oncology nurse now, I realize how frightening it was to have gotten therapy that way. They would just go into the crook of your arm and put it into this nice big fat vein, which would eventually become damaged with scar tissue. Also, many of the chemotherapies back then leaked from the vein into the tissue and skin, which caused a lot of damage to the surrounding skin, often causing it to die. Now we have permanent ports inserted under the skin for receiving an entire amount of chemotherapy, which is much safer.

It's interesting to think about body image. When I was twenty-four, I had a few scars from the biopsies. They had to go into my lungs, so I have a large scar on my chest. They moved my ovaries, so I have a scar in the pelvic region. These are all hide-able scars; I mean they really don't make that much difference at all. But they're there. Sometimes the little tattoo marks that were left from targeting the radiation make more of a difference to me than those other scars, because people would ask, "What are those? You've got these strange blue dots on you. You ought to have those checked out." When you have radiation therapy, they have to be incredibly accurate as to where they aim the ra-diation beams. They tattoo small targets on your body and you have to lie really, really still. If they're on your torso, they're permanent. If they're on your face, they often just draw lines. But many times those tattoos will be permanent, too. If you have a good technician doing this tattooing, they can be really accurate and make tiny, tiny, tiny little dots that most people won't notice. But after treatment, they ask that you keep these tattoos permanently. That way, if you do have a recurrence, they can see exactly where your treatment field was. Well, the person who was doing mine got a little bit messy, and the dots kind of spread out. And so, fifteen years later, I had these three pretty large blue tattoos. A radiation oncologist who I actually worked with at one of the cancer centers in Tucson said that they could be removed now. He removed some of the tattoos that were showing a little bit at my neckline. But most people live with their tattoos for the rest of their lives.

But I'll tell you, as a young adult who had a cancer history when nobody really knew how to deal with me and consequently lost my ability to have children, the internal emotional scarring was much more of a problem for me than the external scarring. The internal scarring made tremendous differences in how I viewed and consequently presented myself when it came to relationships. Even if I was in a relationship, if I had a boyfriend and he didn't care about the external scars, I still felt bad about myself. I felt like damaged goods. I felt like an incomplete package. Why would anyone want to get involved with me when they could just as easily get involved with somebody who could give them children? It did affect many relationships that I had. I think that this is one of the areas that we have much more information on now. With the type of psychosocial support we have available, we can address these kinds of issues with the young-adult and young-adolescent survivors. We can say, "These may be the kind of issues we need to talk about in a group of young adults. Let's talk about sex and the single survivor." I get questions all the time from young adults when I give presentations: "When do you tell people that you have cancer? Do you tell them right up front? Do you wait until you develop a relationship?" For many of us, the whole socialization-after-cancer thing is a huge issue. It's sometimes a larger issue than having experienced and gotten through the life-threatening disease and the treatment itself.

Back in the mid-'70s, in my hometown, there were no such things as support groups. When I started working as an oncology nurse, I ended up being the support for a lot of my patients. But I burned out after a couple of years, because I was supporting and supporting and supporting and giving out all of this energy with nothing coming back in to me. I eventually did seek out some help. I saw a psychiatrist at one time. I've seen psychologists and social workers. But at that time, there weren't specialized oncology support groups, and they really didn't know how to deal with those of us who had survived cancer. So I never really had much resolution as a result of the limited support that I got early on. Now we have specialists in these areas who know exactly how to deal with different populations, people going through different stages of the disease and people in different age and social groups.

It's been interesting going to the retreats and workshops that I've participated in and helped to coordinate over the years. Some of the most interesting and requested sessions deal with sexuality and relationship issues. The issues vary depending on the age, gender, cancer, and treatment. The younger survivors are often dealing with a lot of emotional and social issues, like "How do I actually relate to people? How do I become involved with my peers who don't understand what I'm going through? What about those who may not want to touch me because they're afraid I might be contagious?" That myth is still very viable today. "Why would anyone want to get involved with a person who may have another episode of cancer? Why would they want to get involved with me, when it could come back and I could die?" I think a lot of younger people just don't have the coping skills to deal with a lot of those issues. So we see a lot of those problems.

Females of any age, who have had any kind of gynecologic cancer requiring major surgery to the pelvic area, may have literal physical reasons why they have problems with a sexual relationship. Some younger patients go into premature menopause because of therapy, and they have tremendous problems, both emotionally and physically. They have tremendous problems with sexual intimacy. Some people can be given hormone-replacement therapy to alleviate these symptoms, but others can't. So that really sets up a whole different issue.

And then there are many men who have problems as a result of their radiation. For men who have had testicular cancer or prostate cancer, or any cancer where they've had a focused treatment in the pelvic region, there is the potential for having some kind of a problem like low sperm count or erectile dys-function. These are all very real and important issues.

Now we've got organizations, like Fertile Hope, that make information available to people so that they can start dealing with their potential issues hopefully before they even start their treatment. I think sexual dysfuction is an issue for which we really need to start referring people to specialists. Then they can identify whether it's a physical, psychological, or social problem (or a combination), and help people deal with it and find some alternatives or some kind of resolution with which people can live for the rest of their lives. It's important not to minimize it as "just a problem" because, after all, they've survived cancer.

I got this line: "We've cured you. What more do you want?" Those exact words were actually said to me when I was twenty-four, had just been told I had Hodgkin's, and my entire life was ahead of me. I had hoped to marry and have a family. That was what we did back then. Today it's still a lot of young people's hope and dream to have children. I sat in my room for three days crying after the physician said I was going to start chemotherapy that was going to make me infertile. He deliv-ered the news and just turned around and walked out of the room. And I sat there and cried for three days. Nobody wanted to come near me. I was in a veteran's hospital because I had been a nurse in the army. I was a young woman in the VA with cancer. They didn't have a clue as to what to do with me. So for three days I was very, very weepy and I couldn't figure it out for myself. Why am I crying? It was that loss of fertility. As a young adult, that was my loss, that was my greatest loss.

When the physician finally came back three days later, he said, "Well, what more do you want? We're going to cure you." I suppose it was his way of trying to make it all right for me. But he didn't know what to say to me, being a young guy him-self. Now we've got nurses, other survivors, psychologists, and social workers, who come in and sit and talk about what this kind of a loss at such a young age does to a person. They rec-ognize that this is very important to the patient, and that even though they may have been given their life back, it doesn't mean that they can't grieve the losses they're experiencing.

I'm so thrilled to have been and continue to be a part of the very beginning movement of cancer advocacy. In October of 1986, I was very fortunate to be involved in a meeting in Albuquerque, New Mexico. I was a substitute for another oncology nurse survivor who couldn't make it. It was so fortuitous that I was the one who went, because it's where we formed the National Coalition for Cancer Survivorship. I was so overwhelmed by the people who had gathered in this room. They were all doing exciting things in the field of supporting people with cancer, increasing their quality of life. I sat there and breathed a sigh of relief. I thought, "Here's a group of people who understand what I've been going through and who understand my issues. They see them as relevant and important."

At the meeting, we discussed who our constituency was. We began to discuss, "Well, who's a cancer survivor?" The insurance companies are the ones who first coined the term "cancer survivor." Cancer survivors were the people who were left behind when the patient died, because back then everybody who had cancer died from it. But we'd come a long way since then. All of a sudden we had this ray of hope that there were treatments that could possibly cure some people with cancer. This was totally new back in the late '60s, early '70s. The medical community then said to us, "If you live cancer-free for five years, we pretty much think that you are going to be okay and be out of the woods and that your disease will be gone." So for five years, people were tiptoeing around on eggshells waiting for that magic five-year mark.

Well, as time went on, we realized that there were some people who would never have the opportunity to get to five years. There were some people who thought that their disease was cured after five years and then had a recurrence six, seven, eight years later. So we said, "Gosh, this five-year thing really doesn't work for us as a group." There were health-care professionals and consumer advocates and survivors all sitting around, and we came at it from a more philosophical point of view. "Cancer survivors really start their journey from the day they hear they are diagnosed. We are all cancer survivors." It was certainly a better way of looking at the whole scenario than calling ourselves "cancer victims." We hated the term "victim," because it meant we had absolutely no control and that our quality of life was totally hit-or-miss. We needed to really take some control. Even though we may not be able to control the cancer, we can control the way we deal with it and the way we live the rest of our lives. So we decided that we would all be cancer survivors from the moment of diagnosis forward.

Then we decided to extend "cancer survivor" to the other people who are affected by cancer. Our family members are affected by cancer. Our friends, our employers, our health-care providers, everybody is affected in some way. We began to look at the word "survivor" as more of an overarching definition. And that's where we came up with the concept of survivorship. Survivorship is a process, not a stage. Survivorship is a journey that starts when we hear we're diagnosed and that ends when we die, because cancer has now become a permanent part of our lives.

Even though we have so much more available—resources, Web sites, hotlines, books, and publications—not all of it is in one place, and rarely does anything focus on life after treatment. It's terrifying when it's all over, because now you've got to learn how to be a survivor all on your own. That chemotherapy, that radiation therapy, and whatever else that was treating you and helping to keep it all under control, is gone. So we go off therapy with such conflicted feelings. Learning how to balance these fears and anxieties with a hopefulness of living without cancer is a very difficult transition for many of us.

Sharing information will further the arena of healthy survivorship, of good-quality-of-life survivorship. It will certainly give people something to be hopeful for and let them know that somebody still cares about them even though their treatment is over. A lot of survivors say, "I'm so glad that somebody still cares about me, even though it's five, ten, fifteen years later." Survivors very often don't feel like they should be making any demands or requests, because they've lived this long; they don't want to whine about problems because they're long-term survivors, for which they are grateful. Yet there are people out there who need continued support. They are having a whole new set of problems, and we need to let them know that if something happens to them, if they have a symptom, if they experience any employment discrimination, if they can't get a divorce because they'll lose their insurance, if they're starting to have some kind of anxieties or post-traumatic stress disorder, there's a place where they can find information and support, reassurance that these problems and issues are perfectly normal and that help is available.

I'm Susan Leigh. I'm a thirty-two-year survivor of Hodgkin's disease and then later breast and bladder cancer.

Live strong.

Acknowledgments

The Lance Armstrong Foundation would like to say thank you to the thousands of cancer survivors who shared their stories with us. Your spirit and honesty move us to do the best work we can, every day.

We also express our thanks to the family and friends of those survivors for providing care and comfort to your loved ones; you continue to inspire us

to the entire staff and board of the Lance Armstrong Foundation for your brilliant ideas, your energy, and your commitment to cancer survivors everywhere

to the Lance Armstrong Foundation's community and research partners for your unifying work to provide cancer survivors with the support that they need

to Tiffany Galligan for your tireless leadership and direction on this project and to Nancy Tran for helping to find and recruit cancer survivors to share their stories

to Alpheus Media for your amazing work filming cancer survivors' stories with sensitivity and affection

to Kendra Harpster for being a kind and compassionate editor and never losing sight of the soul of each survivor who shared his or her story

and, finally, to Lance Armstrong for his unending passion and commitment to the cancer community.

About the Foundation

The Lance Armstrong Foundation believes that in the battle against cancer, unity is strength, knowledge is power and attitude is everything. From the moment of diagnosis, the foundation provides the practical information and tools that people with cancer need to live strong. The foundation was founded in 1997 by cancer survivor and cycling champion Lance Armstrong. The foundation is located in Austin, Texas.

www.lancearmstrong.com
www.laf.org
www.livestrong.org

More great books from Bantam

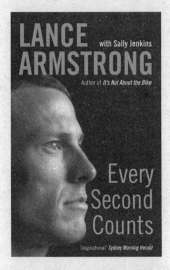

The much-anticipated sequel to the international bestseller, *It's Not About the Bike*, by cancer survivor and six-time Tour de France winner Lance Armstrong.

Moving, down-to-earth, funny and inspiring, this extraordinary story of a single mother who triumphed over impossible odds would be compelling even if bestselling author and six-time Tour de France winner Lance Armstrong wasn't her son.

Available from all good bookshops